ON THE EATIN' PATH

A very biased dining guide to the Rogue Valley and beyond.
52 weeks - 52 adventures

AMAYA • GRILLO • SCHNEIDER

ISBN 0-9634018-4-X

At this crazy time in history,
the world and its inhabitants
are suffering from an obvious
lack of love. This book was
written as a joyous celebration
of love which we offer to you —
to change the balance of things
just a little.

from Margaret Dials

Dedicated to
our children,
our parents,
our families,
our friends,
and pets.

ACKNOWLEDGMENTS

We want to specifically acknowledge and thank these beings for contributing to our success in producing this book. They might have done one or all of the following at one time or another in these last 18 months: offered emotional, financial, physical support, provided child and pet care, chauffeured, proof-read, edited, commented, gave opinions, inspired, shared hot tips, found a swamp cooler on a 110-degree day, encouraged, shared meals, offered advice, dispensed comfort, and believed in us.

David and Ingrid Amaya
Lois and Reuben Amaya
Stefano and Deborah Anderson
Lynn Andreoli-Woods
Aunt Judy
Judy Backen
Captain Coconut
Margaret, Elizabeth, Amy Dials
Denise and Lorene Elzea
Leatrice Goodwin
The Girls: Susie, Annie, Nancy, Catherine
Joe, Anthony, Chris, Nick,
   Vince and Aunt Mary Grillo
Linda Hatch
Loren Heueritz
Bob, Eleanor, Barbara, Beverly, Robby Hills
Andrew Huston
Marie, David, Paul, Gordon Irvine
Corrine Jennings
Jennyratts
Marvin Kaphan
Geoffrey Lewis

Lizzie
Bob Lynn
Virginia Lyon
Yoshinori Murakami
Nanie and Grandpa Hollands
Bozhi Nevada
Kathy Niskanen
Engrique Olguin
Connie, Keith, Steven Pendleton
Michael Ross
Marion Sasaki
Jeff and Dawn Schneider
Jim and Jennifer Scott
Stan Scovell
Janet Souza
Heather Thomas
David Thornton
Karen Valdes
Denie, Tom, Daniel, Jed, Scott Weaver
JoJo Welch
Kerrin White

HOW DO YOU USE THIS BOOK?

The restaurants are listed alphabetically in the Tables of Contentment. In the Index, they are categorized by Bargains, Fine Dining, Vegetarian, Locations (including those within walking distance of Shakespeare), Excursions (with notes especially for tourists), etc. Each article highlights ʕ ʕ our biases. At the end of each one, we give some capsule information that will help you plan a visit: hours, reservation suggestions (only if needed), alcohol served or not, credit cards accepted or not, and where to park.

A note about the meal prices you'll find: we have rounded them to the nearest dollar or half-dollar. Although we were as accurate as possible in collecting our information, please be aware that costs may, like Oregon weather, change quickly. If you're in doubt about this, or any other information, give the restaurant a call before you leave home. Hours especially are subject to change, and particularly in the winter.

We are looking forward to your comments and suggestions, so we have included a response form following the Index. Let us know about your biases in restaurants and food, and your opinions of this book.

About the adventure of new restaurants and dishes, we have a story: One year we hosted a Japanese teacher and he prepared traditional dishes each week for some third- and fourth-grade friends. They devoured chicken livers and gizzards in onion, garlic, and shoyu, oxtails, vegetables with seaweed, and fish sauces. Yoshi's success lay in not acknowledging their food phobias or hesitancy. Each dish was simply "a Japanese secret, good for you." They invariably asked for seconds and tried to wangle another invitation to dinner. We found his advice worked for trying new restaurants, so our tires often squealed and the babies and doggies held on as we dove into parking lots or side roads in search of the next unique dining experience.

WHAT CRITERIA DID WE USE FOR SELECTING RESTAURANTS?

We arrived anonymously, usually with companions, ate and enjoyed our meals, paid for them, and asked for no special treatment. Later, we interviewed and compiled notes. We did not set out to give stars or critique white sauces. We took notice of a recurring pattern of how we intuitively discussed and chose restaurants: a great view, the dessert tray, simple steaks, bargains, a drive and a meal, something non-fattening or healthy, a night on the town, takeout, the chef or proprietor, singing birds or bubbling streams, ethnic, atmosphere, a craving of some kind...

We realized that this conveniently divided restaurants into categories that we called "unique," according to our biases. We also noticed that these categories had the common theme of comforting some want, desire, or need. And so something about these restaurants reassured us in some way.

As Judith Olney, in Comfort Foods, explains: "There are, therefore, physical characteristics and visual appearances largely shared among all categories of food...The sensuous aspects of comforting foods, if I can be forgiven for scrambling them together, revolve around creaminess, smoothness, gold, amber, brown, dapples, speckles, lumps, chunks, plumpness, wholeness, juiciness, aroma, fullness, expansiveness, abundance, repletion....sharing itself should be the final goal of all comforting foods, sharing from the same source, partaking together of heat and sustenance, and so...presents a series of participation dishes wherein each guest must break a piece from the whole or stir a final seasoning into his dish and thereby involve himself, if only symbolically, in the task of preparation as well as the final act of eating."

WHERE DID WE FIND THESE RESTAURANTS?

We concentrated on the Rogue Valley (Ashland, Medford, Talent, Jacksonville, Grants Pass), and we chose some very special restaurants located in outlying areas, including Northern California.

WHEN DID WE WRITE THIS BOOK?

It all began in our hearts and stomachs over 25 years ago when we worked as waitresses to finance our teenage desires, then it grew to meeting over chips, salsa, and beer at secretarial lunches in an L.A. dive. Soon we moved up to meeting in the Mission District at the Marathon Cafe, the oldest Greek restaurant in Los Angeles, where, following our first dinner, we were so overcome that we actually left without paying, and were pursued down the sidewalk by our worried waiter. So it went, and so it goes.

But the formal writing began in January 1991. In the last three months before publication, we revisited every place that had not been on our regular standby list and we encountered new ones that were repeatedly recommended.

A final word of caution: often we wrote during late-night hours, since the kids (though not the hamsters) were asleep. Errors may have crept in, and we do apologize.

WHY ON EARTH DID WE WRITE THIS BOOK?

M.F.K. Fisher, the eloquent writer of essays, recipes and food books, has said: "It seems to me that our three most basic needs, for food and security and love, are so mixed and mingled and entwined that we cannot straightly think of one without the others. So it happens that when I write of hunger, I am really writing about love....Sharing food with another human being is an intimate act that should not be indulged in lightly. There are few people alive with whom I care to pray, sleep, dance, sing, or share my bread and wine."

We don't want to tell you where not to eat, or what to eat. We simply want to share the fun and adventure we've had. We hope to enhance one of the common threads that draws us all together — the experience of dining.

WHO WROTE THIS BOOK AND WHOSE BIASES ARE THESE?

Amaya is also known as the Deb in Deb, Dog & Kid. She attributes her dining-out dedication to working at the International House of Pancakes in Granada Hills, California. When it opened in the early 60's, the neighborhood moms and their teenage kids became the complete IHOP staff: waitresses, cooks, hostesses, bus boys, dishwashers. She especially liked the uniform: teacup of a hat, orange dress, brass belt, white apron, and collar with large brown bow (colors coordinated to the IHOP decor). This is believed to be a reversion to her Brownie and Girl Scout days. Her comfort foods (all Mom's specialties) include hamburger gravy on toast, tuna sandwiches, well-done toast, vegetable soup served with lemon and raisin-walnut bread (to be enjoyed while watching a Johnny Weissmuller Tarzan movie) and her Nanie's beans and hamhocks with onions and vinegar. Mom continues to maintain the family's financial solvency by waitressing and presently works at Emilia's, but that is NOT the only reason to go there. Amaya particularly thanks Alexandra, David, Lani, Margaret, Mary, her family here and in Atchison, Kansas, and her dog Lizzie, who waited while everyone ate.

Grillo answers the phone for Anthony, Christopher, Nick, Vince and Joe. She stands out in her friends' minds for wearing a large, glazed doughnut on the seat of her pants. She admits the experience humbled her. Although usually quite modest, she does proudly acknowledge that she has managed not to lose her 1972 Westchester High School ring. She grew up in L.A. where she loved the Mongolian and Woody's Barbeque Restaurants. At the latter, she could create her own ice cream sundaes, with 95% fudge and cherries. Her mom used to fix her sandwiches with cardboard cutouts of ham that said, "I love you." Grillo's comfort foods include artichokes with mayonnaise (50-50), her mom's moo-shoo pork, and her grilled English muffins with sharp cheese, bacon, and garden tomatoes. She despises peas, but eats exactly 10 when they are served, to set a virtuous example. Grillo (the artist) draws a parallel between playing golf and eating at a restaurant. In both cases, she feels she's in a surreal bubble, removed from ordinary life, enjoying her surroundings, companions, and the sport at hand. She thanks Beverly, Barbara, and Robby Hills for keeping the memories alive — her mom, who taught them how to give without losing themselves, in addition to being the wind beneath their wings — and her dad for his legacy of charm and humor. She also thanks Joe for his undying, although dwindling, support.

All three authors thank her dad for the magical Macintosh!

Schneider, AKA Yani or Auntie, resides in Glendale, California, until she **can't take it anymore!** Then she heads for the Rogue Valley or Italy, whichever grabs her fancy or whichever her pocketbook can afford. Ignoring the best advice of Consumer Reports, she prefers to eat her comfort foods while lying under an electric blanket. Among these favorites are pound cake with heavy cream, Japanese noodle soup with egg and sesame oil, Grandmother's Christmas cookies, mashed potatoes with chopped white onion, soup with barley, and homemade biscuits with jam. Her current craze is Thai cuisine, which she may even cook from time to time. She avoids green peppers and okra, but all other food items are fair game. However, as of the publication of this book, she is seriously considering dieting. She has often been teased about her dog, J. Ratts, who is always fed perfectly microwaved and gently stirred food, and who is sometimes found standing on the Schneider dining table. She gives special thanks to Jeff, for steadfast support, and to Deborah and Mary, for making this book a reality.

TABLES OF CONTENTMENT

Alex's Plaza Restaurant & Bar 1

Applegate River Ranch House 3

Arbor House Restaurant 6

Ashland Soy Works 8

Bagel Man 12

Beasy's Back Room 14

Beckie's Café 16

Bel Di's on the Rogue 18

Bloomsbury Books and Coffee House 20

Breadboard Restaurant and Bakery 22

Britt Landing 24

Brothers' Restaurant & Delicatessen 28

Buckhorn Springs 30

C.K. Tiffin's 32

Café 24 34

Campers Cove Restaurant 36

Chata 38

China Station 40

Emelia's 42

The Good Bean 44

Goodtimes 47

Great American Pizza Company 49

Hamilton House 51

Harmony Natural Foods and Café 54

House of Thai Cuisine 57

Hyatt Lake Resort 59

Il Giardino Cucina Italiana 61

Jacksonville Inn Bistro and Bar 63

TABLES OF CONTENTMENT

La Burrita Restaurant and Delicatessen 65

Lithia Park/Winter Café 67

Manna Bakery 69

Maria's Mexican Kitchen 71

Markisio's 73

Matsukaze Japanese Cuisine 76

McCully House Inn 79

Mihama Teriyaki/Grill 81

Morrison's Lodge 83

Munchies of Ashland 87

Nature's Kitchen 89

New Sammy's Cowboy Bistro 91

North Light Vegetarian Restaurant 94

Omar's Restaurant and Bar 97

Pinehurst Inn at Jenny Creek 100

Pongsri's Thai-Chinese Cuisine 102

Primavera Restaurant & Gardens 104

R-Haus Restaurant 106

Renate's Alpine Restaurant & Bar 109

Rogue Brewery and Public House 111

Samovar Family Restaurant and Bakery 113

Sengthong's 116

Serge's 119

Sunshine Natural Foods Cafe 122

Index 125

Response Form 130

Order Form 132

Alex's Plaza Restaurant & Bar

35 N. Main Street, on the plaza
Ashland • 482-8818

Alex wants people to come in and have a nice time. It's easy to oblige. The bar is large and usually packed with a friendly combination of people, from tourists to Shakespearean theater actors. As Alex says, his place is unpretentious with a casual atmosphere, "But," he adds, "we take care of business." Reservations are recommended, especially in summer.

Alex used to own a restaurant called the Mountain House on a little ridge-top right where the redwoods begin, south of San Francisco. The ocean was on one side, the bay on the other. He sometimes gets customers from the old place, stopping in, people on the run, like him, from the Silicon Valley atmosphere. He loves Ashland and the whole idea of tourists coming up to enjoy theater —they're mellow and ready to relax, eat, and stroll around the area. Contrast this to the frazzled tourists at, ummm, let's say Disneyland on a hot, smoggy weekend in Orange County.

If music be the food of love, play on ... Shakespeare

Cinco de Mayo is a special day of celebration for Alex — on that day, five years ago, his restaurant opened in Ashland. This second story, which houses the roomy bar and large dining room, was added to the Perrine Building, the first brick structure in town, around 1900. Alex hates dark bars and air conditioning, so when he saw this old building with its spaciousness and high ceilings, he knew he had something. The brick walls and fir floors were restored, and lots of skylights added. Past the dining room is the deck (overlooking Guanajuato Way and Lithia Creek) where the club and dinner menus are served. Although he added the two fireplaces and the front bar, it's impossible to find a break in the overall harmony.

 **Bar ∎ club menu ∎ outside dining!**

Lunch and dinner are served six days a week. Monday is dinner only. The club menu ($2-7.50) includes inventive appetizers, seafood, pasta, Tuscan stew, chicken wings, and sandwiches plus their savory house pizza: pesto, pine nuts, cheese, and oregano. You can order from the club menu in the bar and on the deck, weekdays till 10 and weekends until midnight. It's perfect for the after-theatre munchies.

I only drink to make other people interesting.   G. J. Nathan

The dinner menu reflects local favorites and specialties like the horseradish that grows in Tule Lake. Selections usually include two fresh fish choices, chicken, ribs, veal, game hen, steak, pasta, and lamb ($15-22).

Every Sunday, a jazz and rag pianist entertains the bar crowd. Jazz is scheduled for parties and holidays like Halloween, July 4, Cinco de Mayo, St. Patrick's, and New Year's. Some time ago, Alex's had a reputation for its jazz entertainment, but Alex got burned out on all the scheduling, although he still talks about Humphrey, the sax player from New Orleans. It got too cold for Humphrey, but when he returns Alex has a spot for him.

We have a favorite memory of this place. A few summers ago, a sudden storm blew in, so we took refuge on the small balcony off the bar. Overlooking the plaza, Main Street and the mountains beyond, we watched the rain and sipped our drinks in a moment of pure contentment.

•M 5-10, Tu-Sun 11:30-9, (midnight on weekends)
• Full bar
• Credit cards
• Park in plaza or city lots

Applegate River Ranch House

15100 Highway 238
Applegate • **846-6082**

A half-hour from Jacksonville, just across from the Applegate store, we left the highway and entered a welcoming area with split-rail fences strung with dainty lights leading to the cedar-fronted restaurant. A 1930 Model A Ford parked beside our car looked perfectly attuned to the place. There were sunny flowers, birds chirping, a pleasant cool bridge in the background, and the wonderful scent of pines. Recent rains had brought out the natural lushness of the riverbanks.

The dining rooms overlook the lazy Applegate. Owners Joanna and Richard Davis have added a new banquet room and a gorgeous, multi-tiered wooden deck -- construction was still underway when we visited. Throughout the comfortable interior are Western artifacts — beautifully tooled leather saddles, lariats, bridles, chaps, tools, portraits of Indians, rodeo and cowboy photographs. Richard races his own horses -- he was in a post-win euphoria when we first met him that evening. Local ranchers bring in their branding irons and leave their marks on the wood ceilings and walls -- branders receive an automatic 15 percent discount.

" Waiter, there's a fly in my soup."
" Now there's a fly that knows good soup."

Second oldest fly joke.

We were early enough to capture seats at the window, and we settled in appreciatively at the candle-lit, blue-draped table. Our server, a struggling nursing student, dispensed menus and tiny half-pineapple wooden bowls filled

 **Atmosphere ▪ award-winning food!**

with fresh pineapple and tangy mint. Our mouths awoke and our eyes lit up. Eureka! Aloha! We have cowboy — we have Hawaii — we have Hawaiian cowboy, or paniolo, as the menu explains. Joanna Davis and chef Duke Gima, we learn, are from Hawaii, and the rancher themes and tastes of Island and Valley mesh here at Applegate.

The award-winning specialties of the house are meat, fish, and poultry grilled over red oak brought in from Northern California. After prolonged and rapacious perusal of menu choices, we summoned the waitress; changed our orders several times, and leaned back with a sigh.

I choose my friends as I choose my food.

Anonymous

Promptly our appetizers arrived. The four of us jockeyed indelicately for possession of the oak-grilled mushrooms, marinated in oilve oil, basil, lemon juice, and garlic ($3.50); and the half-bucket of tender steamers ($6) with Chardonnay, garlic, and shallots. We considered asking for straws to sip the broth, but settled on thick hunks of bread.

Salad was a pleasing array of crisp greens with (of course) ranch dressing, and deliciously bite-y bleu cheese crumbled overtop. The soup du jour was Portugese bean, traditional Hawaiian, with chunks of Portugese sausage, red kidney beans, cabbage, thick and richly seasoned. Our entrées were served and almost simultaneously made to vanish. There were (fleetingly) grilled tuna with Bercy (clarified, herby) and pineapple salsa butters ($13); rack of lamb Provencal, redolent with garlic, spiced with mint ($17); and juicy chicken breasts, oaky, with an aroma of rosemary ($8). The four-inch-tall Hula pie, split four ways, vanquished us completely. We realized there are steaks, prawns ("angels on horseback"), a vegetarian plate, paniolo ribs and more to sample. Starry-eyed with gratitude, we sipped our coffee and shared a moment with Richard Davis, who stopped by our table to make sure we were happy. We asked if the place was always this full, and he laughed out loud. Yes — and today's the Blazers' championship, he said. We had completely forgotten. He talked about future plans — finishing the decks, planning the children's games (horseshoes, lawn-washers) for the summer on the front lawn and horseback riding in the area across the parking lot.

Suddenly there was a rising swell of excited voices, and all heads swiveled towards the window and the Applegate. Several of us rushed out onto the deck. Across the river, a large wise-eyed raccoon sat dipping his catch into the water and — we would swear to it — gave us a wink.

- Daily 5—9
- Reservations suggested
- Beer, wine
- Credit cards
- Park in lot

Arbor House Restaurant

103 West Wagner
Talent • 535-6817

The Arbor House is a simply exquisite place to dine — superb dishes placed like jewels in a setting made to order.

You enter under a wooden archway and pass through a small, perfect garden where a stream flows peacefully beneath a tiny bridge. The lattice-covered walls of the house are feathered with climbing plants. The interior room is welcoming, with an entire wall covered floor to ceiling with photographs of friends and family. We choose the outdoor screened patio when we can, to watch the sun set. There are thick, warm sweaters hung on the chair backs, in case you're chilly after nightfall.

Happy is the man possessing the superior holy blessing of a judgement and taste — accurate, refined and chaste.

Aristophanes

The menu is an international tour, first class. From India, there are curried entrées of chicken, lamb, beef, or seafood. You can order them mild, medium, or spicy, and your server will bring you a sample as it's cooking to make sure it's exactly to your liking. Our choice arrived with side dishes of coconut, sunflower seeds, yogurt, and homemade cranberry chutney. There's lamb from Great Britain, sauerbraten, beef stroganoff, chicken enchilada, Italian scampi, jambalaya, steaks, and Caesar salad.

There are specials every night, like the fresh (delivered two hours before) halibut, baked and served with a Provencal butter (bay shrimps, tomato, lemon, garlic, parsley), or tomato-basil chicken breasts sautéed in white wine, cream, oregano, basil, and fresh tomatoes.

 Gourmet food ■ lovely surroundings ■ personal service!

The menu comes without prices but feel free to ask — the usual range is $11-15. Dinner includes soup with airy biscuits; salad of red cabbage, romaine, red leaf lettuce, bean and alfalfa sprouts and cucumber; or the Greek salad. Three very different salad dressings accompany them and we tried them all: creamy yogurt (with oil, vinegar, tarragon, poppyseed, caraway, and dill); tomato-honey (spicy with garlic, hot mustard, red wine vinegar); and the Dijon poppyseed (mustard, honey, oil, vinegar, Worchestershire, and white pepper). Garlic bread absorbed the final spoonfuls. Many of the herbs are grown in the garden to the rear, or just outside the brushwood gate.

Homemade desserts one recent visit encompassed strawberry shortcake, New York-style raspberry cheesecake, and ice cream cakes ($3-3.50).

The Calhoun family are the guiding lights of Arbor House. We were served by owner Kitty and son, Eric, whose attentive service and unpretentious manner were a delight. They don't like to turn anyone away, so be kind enough to make reservations.

- **•Tu-Sat 5-9 (winter W-Sat)**
- **• Reservations suggested**
- **• Beer, wine**
- **• No credit cards**
- **• Park in lot**

Ashland Soy Works

225 Water Street
Ashland •482-1865

From Main, take Water Street downhill (how else can water run?) past the Rogue Brewery and through a squeezy mini-tunnel that looks like an irrigation pipe. Bear left and watch out for the city trucks backing up (beep-beep-beep) and the John Deere earth-moving equipment. Across from the recycling center, in an environmentally impeccable area, is the Ashland Soy Works.

There are determined flowers in a rock-strewn bed, a few picnic tables on a lattice-shaded patio, and a miniature building. Inside, there are three elfen tables, flanked by shelves of ceramic bowls, plates, cups — the cupboard-sized Clouded Mountain Ceramics Gallery.

An empty stomach is not a good political advisor. Albert Einstein

Friendly folk service the counter to your left. Everything is fresh, whole-some and nonboring. From noon to five on weekdays, you may order tofu with ginger, hot tofu loaf on a roll with marinara and cheese, burritos with sautéed tofu and vegetables in whole-wheat tortillas, juicy with salsa, sprouts and sour cream — a three-napkin delight. The pita bread sandwich is stuffed liberally with ginger-spiced baked tofu, brown rice and olives. Salads are sprightly and riotous with color. There are tasty fruit cheesecakes and honey-soy vanilla shakes for sin-free enjoyment.

 Amazingly yummy good-for-you food ■ art gallery!

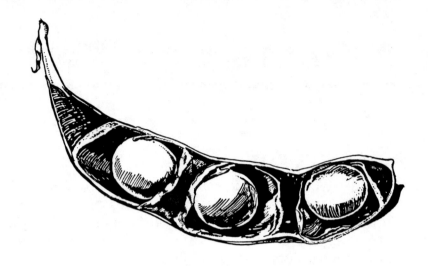

Soy Works supplies goods to many local establishments and does a steady volume of take-out business, but visitors should be aware of these light, delicious, inexpensive, vegetarian meals. Five dollars will satisfy your tastebuds completely, and leave your pockets jingling with change.

Good, when communicated, more abundant grows.
Albert Einstein

Diana and Jim Muhs have been making tofu here for more than ten years. She's a true believer in the versatility of this wonder food, sponsors cooking classes, and will be more than pleased to share recipes.

For those unfamiliar with this I-can-be-anything substance, we offer the following true/false quiz:

1. Soybeans can be baked.
> True. Also, they can be fermented for sauce and tofu can be sautéed, steamed, or smoked.

2. Tofu comes from soybeans.
> True. The beans are soaked and steamed into a mash, and the soy milk is turned into curds by the addition of of nigari, a seawater coagulant. Curds are strained, pressed and packaged — voilá — tofu!

9

3. Soy is relatively new.

False. The Chinese have used this "yellow jewel" for thousands of years.

4. Beer might be made with soy products; so might fire extinguishers.

True. The extinguisher might use soy protein in its foam and some beers employ soy meal in brewing.

5. Soybeans are high in fat.

False. They have less fat than any other protein source. They are higher in protein though, more than any other crop.

6. Miso is unrelated to tofu.

False. They're both a chip off the same bean. Miso is fermented soy paste.

7. Tofu should be refrigerated.

True. The traditionally processed tofu should be, but the Japanese are now doing some dry-freezing which allows shelving.

8. Corn oil is more plentiful than soy oil.

False.

9. In the U.S. animals eat more soy products than humans do.

True. Most of the country's soy beans are fed to livestock, which are notoriously inefficient protein machines.

10. Soy beans contain almost no starch.

True. French scientists discovered this a hundred years ago and prescribed them for diabetic diets.

11. Henry Ford once made a hood ornament out of soybean-derived plastic.

False. It was a trunk lid and it was very resilient.

12. There are 25,000 tofu shops in Japan.

False. That was in 1987. It's more like 40,000 now.

13. Soybeans are hard to grow.

False. They're a snap. Machines do most of the work, and the beans grow on marginal land.

14. The most successfully introduced soy food in America was soy sauce.

False. Not even close. It's tofu 'ice cream', with sales up 600 percent in a single, two-year period.

15. Minks eat soybeans.

True. With a few modifications and additions, the beans provide great nutrition for hogs, foxes, shrimp, trout, zoo bears, and silkworms — humans, too.

If you have more than 10 correct, you are a genius. If not, you might want to stop by the Soy Works to see what else you can learn.

- M—F 12-5
- No alcohol
- No credit cards
- Park on street

Bagel Man

1461 Siskiyou Boulevard
Ashland • **488-0357**

On the wall above the sink, there's a two-foot-high cartoon with a scraggly couple having this conversation:

"Wow — just got my hand caught in the bagel machine!"

"Which one?"

"Whadya mean, which one? We've only got one bagel machine!"

Well, the Rogue Valley really has only one bagel machine, too, and here it is, tucked into a nondescript shopping center just a few doors from Buy-Rite.

The ovens fire up at 3 am with an average daily output of 3,000 bagels, plus other specialty baked goods. When the doors open in the morning, the rich aroma acts like a magnet on waiting customers. There's a small, pleasant seating area inside or you can easily dash in and pick up an order to go.

The end of labor is to gain leisure ... Aristotle
... so that you can drink coffee ... L. Peter

The founder is David Pinsky, who now handles the wholesale operations. The administrative end is juggled by his wife, Julia Thompson, and the baking is usually accomplished by partner Mitchell Jackson. They've been together about five years and have cultivated a loyal local following.

 **Fresh bagels ■ budget!**

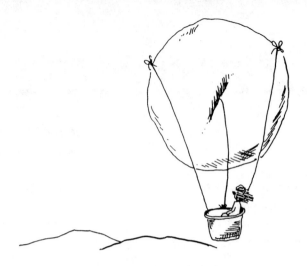

Bagels come in wheat, raisin, sesame, and poppyseed (40 cents) and there's a Power Bagel, thick with oats, raisins, sunflower seeds, and cinnamon for 65 cents. Bagel dogs (turkey) run $1.50, bagelwiches (vegetarian or meat-filled) are $3 and sell out often. There are bagel pizzas, and of course bagels with Nova Scotia lox and cream cheese (about $4). A pastry case displays the day's selection of cookies, muffins, and pretzels, a very popular carrot cake, and if you're lucky, the English hot-cross buns (check Julia's accent). These are delicious, not-too-sweet creations rich with cloves, cinnamon, nutmeg, allspice, and currants — served with coffee from Good Bean. They are a fragrant fantasy.

Hot cross buns,
Hot cross buns,
One-a-penny,
Two-a-penny,
Hot cross buns.
If you have no daughters,
Give them to your sons,
One-a-penny,
Two-a-penny,
Hot cross buns.

• M - F 6:30 — 5; Sat 7 — 2
• No alcohol
• No credit cards
• Park in lot

Beasy's Back Room

139 E. Main Street
Ashland • **482-2141**

Now that Mr. Beasy's Ashland empire is waning, we were anxious to check out the Back Room. It's easy to walk on by if you don't realize it's there — just across from North Light on Main, upstairs behind the China Korea. We met there one recent evening and were pleased to find the new owners, Bruce and Chris Finnie, haven't tampered with the Back Room's most appealing characteristics.

It's still laid-back country style, with plank flooring, an abundance of animal horns, casual wood tables and chairs, and a lonesome cowpoke on the radio. We were there for one of the best-kept bargain secrets around: Openers, served 5:30 to 6 (also known as Closers, from 8:30 to 9). This jim-dandy deal will give you a 6-ounce top sirloin, grilled Texas-style in lemon butter (invariably tender and tasty), grilled onions, hearty German fries, a large green salad with great green-olive special dressing, bread, and a glass of wine or beer. The $8 fee is measly.

Grub first, then ethics.   Bertold Brecht

If you must arrive at the wrong time, the regular menu offers steaks, fresh fish, porkchops, chicken, sausages, shrimp terilingua with pico de gallo, or combinations ($7-15). Kids can order ground sirloin or chicken fillet ($6). Specials on the night of our last visit were grilled halibut ($15), snapper ($12), New York steak ($15), and catfish ($13), with a blackened shrimp appetizer at $7. We never last till dessert, but there are cheesecake and bread pudding for the stout of appetite.

 Reliable steaks ■ budget ■ homey!

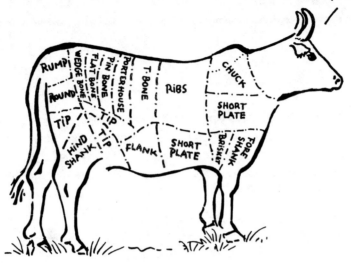

HEY, AM i BEING FiTTED FOR A NEW SUIT?

The Back Room has hosted, and will continue to host, a very special Christmas charity event. Prices are rolled back to a nearly-forgotten historical point — once, four of us dined for 97 cents. The only other payment required is the donation of a Christmas toy for a child.

Hope to see you there!

Some hae meat, and canna eat,
And some wad eat that want it;
But we hae meat and we can eat,
And sae the Lord be thankit.

Robert Burns

- M-Sat 5:30 — 9, Sun 5 — 8:30
- Full bar
- Credit cards
- Park on street

Beckie's Café

Highway 62
Union Creek • **560-3563**

When you mention Beckie's, people nod in acknowledgment and then there's the usual mutual mmm-ing about the pies. And they are justifiably famous. We especially like the very berry and the huckleberry — legends in their own crusts.

One morning not long ago we left Ashland at dawn with the dog and the baby asleep in their carseats and drove out Beckie's way. We stopped in Prospect and walked the leisure path to the Mill Creek falls — the perfect appetite workup. Then 30 minutes later we were seated in one of the cozy crimson booths ordering pancakes and omelets. The Denver ($5) comes with delicate but generous slices of ham that spread the smoked flavor throughout. One time they tried to discourage us from our mission, saying they were out of bell pepper, but we had to have the Denver anyway — it's the ham that makes this dish. Come-withs are pancakes or hashbrowns and toast. Order the homemade bread; it's worth the extra 75 cents.

Who in the hell, I said to myself, wants to try to make pies like Mother makes when it's so much easier to let Mother make them in the first place? **Harriette Arnow**

Another afternoon, with deserving friends in tow, we drove straight to Beckie's for lunch. The Bleu cheeseburger reminds us of the Frenchburgers we used to love at the IHOP. They're juicy, messy, and rich. Other specialty burgers are with bacon and cheese or mushroom and onion and are served with fries for $5. Our youngest friends were happy with their corndog and fries plate ($2). Afterwards, we strolled up the trail that winds back behind Beckie's resort and

 Famous pies ■ excursion ■ recreational area!

cabins, along the river, arriving north of the restaurant at the gorge. By then we had earned our piece of pie — the huckleberry, of course ($2.50). The berries are picked locally (within a 25-mile radius) by natives who know where to look. You won't find them in any market.

The lunch/dinner menu features additional quarter-pound burgers, specialty sandwiches with salad and fries and homemade beef stew with cornbread, all about $5. There are a few mini choices for kids. Dinner entrées, an assortment of steaks, chops, and shrimp ($9-13) are served with potato, soup, or salad and that great bread. Consider the hodge-podge basket, with deep fried mushrooms, cauliflower, cheese sticks, zucchini, and onion rings ($4) — good for sharing a munch.

When you drive here on Highway 62, keep an eye out for the Prospect Ranger Station. They have fine trail maps of this lovely area, and you will want to return. The Natural Bridge is a stone's throw from Beckie's and Mill Creek, and National Creek Falls are just (as our grandad used to say) a hoot and a holler away.

P.S. The name derives from Beckleheimer, the original owner, circa 1926 — we knew you'd be wondering.

- **Till Labor Day: Daily 8—8 (call for winter hours)**
  - **Beer & wine**
  - **Credit cards**
  - **Park in lot**

Bel Di's on the Rogue

21900 Highway 62
Shady Cove • **878-2010**

It was one of those cool, cloudy, just-about-to-rain afternoons that began the summer of 91. We put on our pretty skirts and took a windows-down drive out Crater Lake Highway to meet the Rogue at Bel Di's.

This is a marvelously civilized restaurant. The original structure was built in the thirties and has been serving for six decades, with additions and refinements made over the years.

Entering, you pass through a garden awash in flowers. From the windows of the long, peaceful room, you have a magnificent river view. Voices murmur and wine glasses clink. You feel yourself quieting, listening for the rhythm of the river. In warmer weather, there are two lovely decks to enjoy outside, so close to the Rogue you can almost taste it.

Dinners are served gracefully by local young people, beautifully dressed and mannered. The hospitality is courtesy of Ray and Joan Novosad, who bought Bel Di's in July 1990.

The fish is fresh every night in the summer. That evening, we enjoyed skillfully prepared orange roughy and salmon. The soup was hearty vegetable and the salad had a nice tart vinaigrette. The rice pilaf was light, with pinenuts, celery, and onion. There are baked potatoes, too, and au gratin on Sundays.

Ye diners-out from whom we guard our spoons.
Lord McCauley

The house specialty is stuffed Louisiana prawns ($16) which completely satisfied a friend who spends his days in construction. Other seafood

 Civilized dining with a river view!

choices are scallops, scampi, bass, and halibut ($10-14). Veal and chicken (marsala, polynesian and parmesan) dishes range from $9.50 to 12, steaks from $13-16, and combinations are also served. Prime rib is available every night until it is gone.

There is a separate room for non- smokers. The pleasant bar and lounge to the left of the entrance opens a half-hour before dinner with a limited and less expensive menu and closes in a leisurely fashion.

Desserts are made for dawdling here. There are chocolate mousse and black-berry sundaes but the bread pudding is something special. Our first taste was from the spoon of a reluctant friend —we've learned to order our own now. Relationships have foundered on smaller causes, after all.

Proof of the pudding is in the eating.   Cervantes

Bel Di's is a wonderful setting to relax and enjoy the real star of the show —the Rogue.

•Tu—Sat till 5, Sun 4,
closing whenever, Oregon Standard Time
• Closed last 2 weeks of January
• Reservations suggested, especially for the decks
• Full bar
• Credit cards
• Park in lot

Bloomsbury Books & Coffee House

290 E. Main Street
Ashland • **488-0029**

Our Dad would yell up from the living room, "**Lights out!!!**" Each repitition was at increased volume. When we finally heard him trudging upstairs, we'd snap off the light and fake a dainty snore or two. As soon as he disappeared, the flashlights went on under the covers and we'd finish the chapters we were halfway through Nancy Drew or The Black Stallion Returns. We wonder if Dad ever figured out why all those batteries kept disappearing...

Well, in short, we were reading fanatics even then. Trips to the library were longed-for adventures, and bookstores were an almost aphrodisiac experience. Some things don't change. We were sitting around the table at home the other night, enjoying the grilled snapper our editor and chef had prepared, and musing over the loves of our lives — reading and eating, of course — and how wonderful it is to find a place that combines these two nurturing activities. There were all those cunning hole-in-the-wall spots in Berkeley, where caffeine and politics sparked the air; or Westwood, near the UCLA campus, where students with burdened backpacks would pop in for a croissant and a cram session.

When I get a little money, I buy books.
If there is any left over, I buy food and clothes.
Desiderius Erasmus

The talk that evening naturally turned to Bloomsbury. Out front are racks with the New York Times, Washington Post, and Los Angeles Times. Inside there's the rich world of new books and magazines, a sense of adventures just waiting for the turning of a page. And up the wide wooden stairs, there's a swell little café where your tastes can be happily indulged.

 **Books ■ light fare ■ late night!**

The walls are of friendly old brick, and the half-dozen tables are clustered for convenient eavesdropping, if one is so inclined. Here and on the patio to the rear, regulars congregate daily to snack, play backgammon or chess, peruse the newspaper, finish a novel, write a report, have a debate, skim a magazine article. There's even a little bookcase against the back wall, where you can browse new-book samples from downstairs.

You order at the counter and bus your own plates. Orders are efficiently filled and will satisfy the thriftiest purse at $3-5 per dish. We met one recent night to share the vegetable lasagne, light as angelfood; the Marsala Dosa, a sort of rice-flour tortilla filled with curried, steaming potatoes and onions, with a black bean-coconut chutney. Both were excellent and flavorful, and we soon moved on to the Indian stir-fry with basmati rice, vegetables and raita (yogurt with cucumber, garlic, and onion); and the chicken quiche, thick with red peppers, olives, jack cheese, spinach, and mozzarella. The fruit salad was perfectly fresh and brimming with the season's best offerings. As a second dessert there was a Swiss parfait (this would be fine for breakfast, too), with granola, nutmeg, cinnamon, fruit, and ricotta. There are coffees, teas, and fresh squeezed juices. For breakfast, you can wake up enjoyably with fresh-baked muffins, scones, bagels, and quiches. Homemade soups for lunch or dinner are a popular year-round draw, hot or cold.

We like browsing at Bloomsbury — it's nourishment for mind and body.

- **M-F 8—midnight, Sat 9—midnight, Sun 10—9 (call for winter hours)**
- **No alcohol**
- **No credit cards**
- **Park on street**

Breadboard Restaurant and Bakery

749 N. Main
Ashland • **488-0295**

Periodically during the last nine years, we've suffered from acute *Breadboard Addiction* — though 'suffered' is perhaps the wrong word. There have been periods of a week or two when we made morning pilgrimages. It's a wonderful place to wake up slowly, munching through a stack of really sour, sourdough pancakes drenched in the house Marionberry or spiced apple syrup. It's easy to forget how beautiful our valley is, and the views from the north and south booths are there to remind us.

Only dull people are brilliant at breakfast.

— Oscar Wilde

The place has a tidy, country look, with antiques staged about and craftsy pieces on the walls. The smoking-permitted center room has a fireplace, and there's a small, bright sunroom added on.

Given the name, it seems strange that not all baked goods are made on the premises. The multi-grain bread is, as well as the sour cream pies, muffins, biscuits and plate-sized cinnamon rolls, just meant for sharing. There's a separate tea list on each table.

Breakfast choices served from 7 to 11 are varied and reasonable, under $6. Currently, we're hooked on the Vegetarian Special ($3.50), a marvelous blend of calico rice, green onion, mushrooms and garlic, sautéed in olive oil and tamari.

 **Breakfast with a view!**

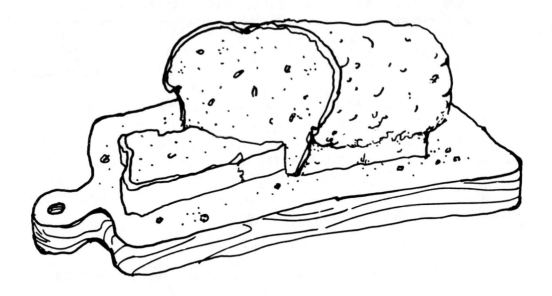

The lunch menu respects the individual appetite. You can mix and match sandwiches, salad, soup, pie. Seven sandwiches come in mini, regular and large sizes, from $2-5, — a thoughtful plus for families.

• M - Sat: 7 - 2:30, Sun: 8 - 2:30
• No alcohol
• No credit cards
• Park in lot

Britt Landing

150 S. Oregon Street
Jacksonville • **899-8248**

Who was C.C. Beekman and what's a coquille? What did Elijah Davidson discover, if not a filet mignon? Was Mary Ann Harris Chambers defending her salmon against an Indian attack? These questions, and many more, can be answered by reading the dinner menu at Britt's Landing. You'll learn more about Mr. Britt himself while you're at it, and the famous Orth Building which houses this restaurant. (The word "orth" has special meaning for us, and whenever we enter the building, we have a good, red-faced laugh. One of our group was a young, naive human geography student at Cal State L.A. when the lesson on latitude and longitude came up. Earnestly completing her homework one night, she located an assigned target in the Orth Sea. This seemed strange at the time; she'd never heard the name of this body of water before; but in her perfectionistic way, against her better instincts, she rechecked the spelling, O-R-T-H, and printed it in her notes. The question was asked in class the very next day and our friend's hand shot up in the air. Divine providence made the professor call on someone else, who gave the correct answer, NORTH Sea. Our friend was thunderstuck. Furtively, blushing scarlet, she checked her atlas. There it was, on the right-hand page, Orth Sea, and on the left page near the center binding, floated the orphan N. The points of the lesson, over time, became clear: Follow your instincts, question authority, realize there's more to any puzzle than might first meet the eye! But back to Jacksonville...)

The historical research on the menu was accomplished by Kathy Hakim, one of the owners who bought the restaurant from Munchies early in 1992 and is busy establishing a new identity for the place. She's a pleasant, obviously action-oriented lady with a ready smile and lots of optimism about her new venture. The setting certainly deserves enthusiasm. This is a gorgeous, upstairs restaurant —

$\widehat{O} \, \widehat{O}$ Atmosphere ■ deck ■ large parties ■ handicapped access ■ spirits!

forest carpets, oak furnishings, airy flowered wallpaper, spacious rooms and tall windows. In front, next to the beautifully panelled new full-service bar, there's a couples-size dining balcony, and at the rear, a roomy redwood patio with a profusion of flowers — this seems to float in the surrounding trees. The deck provides the only wheelchair access in Jacksonville. There's entertainment here Friday and Saturday evenings, as well as Sunday afternoons — great for families. At that time, Herb Wyatt from Grants Pass was playing mellow jazz and folk on acoustic guitar.

When we visited Britt's recently, we were indeed puzzled by the stack of menus (nine in all) that we were given, but we realize Kathy is doing her homework and a more focused bill of fare will surely emerge. Meanwhile, the facts. Corrine and Rebecca do the baking fresh every day, Paul Bunyan pies and other award-winning delicacies.

Breakfast is served Saturday only, starting at 8 am , with a modest selection priced $4-8. On Sundays, the fancy champagne brunch hours are from 10-2 with a limited lunch menu running concurrently after noon. Brunch is $5-11, less for children.

Lunch is served Monday through Saturday from 11 to 3. Creamy clam chowder is the house specialty ($3). There are some nice salads, including Crab Louie ($9), hearty sandwiches ($6-8), as well as pasta, steak, seafood, and kabobs in about the same price range. Kids can dine for $3.50-5 on a few select items.

Everyone to his taste. Plato

Dinner is available from 4:30 to 9 Sunday through Thursday, closing an hour later on Friday and Saturday. Early bird specials (till 6 pm) feature six options at reduced prices, such as scampi or prime rib for $10. The full menu begins with some exciting news — appetizers of fresh oysters ($7) or our happy weakness, fresh roasted garlic ($4), among others. Steaks and prime rib come in regular and he-man portions. There's a rich baked dish of scallops, shrimp, and cheese, or the prawns stuffed with crab and shrimp. The charbroiled chicken is prepared with your choice of three glazes, including tangy lime with basil and oregano. Entrées

include soup or salad, potato or herb rice, and fresh vegetables, and range from $10-18. Desserts change daily, and there's a nice wine selection — dessert wines are being added to the new list. The lounge is open from lunch till the last diners leave, about midnight on weekends. There's a mini-menu of a dozen a la carte lounge choices.

I can resist everything except temptation.

Oscar Wilde

Britt also creates picnic dinners of some of their most popular dishes to take to the theater or any outdoor event. Call to order before noon, please. Weekend reservations for summer dinners are probably a good plan as well.

A last historical note: the J. Orth Building (1872) once housed a brothel, among other businesses, and no one knows just exactly which ghosts linger on. Several former employees agreed that there definitely have been spirits about, though — nothing scary, really, just disconcerting. At the wait station, the ice has been known to make a clatter falling into the metal container — but there's no ice. Beer and wine taps — all in a row — have suddenly gushed — with no one around. One waitress told of being alone after hours, vacuuming, when loaves of bread leaped to the floor. No one's worried though — it's such a pretty place to haunt.

• See hours above
• Reservations suggested
• Full bar
• Credit cards
• Park on street or in Britt lot

Brothers' Restaurant & Delicatessen

95 N. Main Street
Ashland • **482-9671**

There's simply no alternative for New York-Kosher style deli foods — you'd have to drive to San Francisco, and you probably wouldn't find these prices. There are homemade cheese blintzes ($6), lox with cream cheese and bagels ($7.50), borscht ($4), pickled herring ($5.50), potato pancakes ($5), and fried matzo with eggs ($5). The only touches missing are the Brooklyn accents and taxicabs honking.

Brothers' became a community member in 1976 and for the past 11 years has been under the loving stewardship of owner Bob Evaniuk. He credits the longevity of his place to the loyalty of his customers. Ashlanders are the core of his business, but his weekly regulars drive in from Medford and Klamath Falls, too. Families who visit the area each summer turn up year after year and Bob watches their kids grow up. He's a thoughtful person and makes very careful choices about staff and menu. "In a restaurant, it's the intangibles that are important," he says. "The people who work here love it — they have to — and many have been with me five to seven years. If you can't enjoy what you do, it's not worth it — everyone loses, and especially the customer." Bob's menu is extensive but he's wary of trendiness. New dishes are offered as experiments — daily specials — and proven before they're elevated to menu status.

The way to a man's heart is through his stomach. - S. P. Parton

Breakfast at Brothers' is a real crowd-pleaser, and on a recent morning the place filled to capacity in the space of a half-hour. They have beans for breakfast, and we can never resist. They're plump, moist, and soul-satisfying,

 **Deli food ■ member-of-the-family feeling!**

and come with spine-tingling salsa. We ate them with the day's special, a tofu scramble bursting with fresh veggies. The portions are more than a sane person would normally consume, but they don't mind providing an extra plate for two.

Breakfast is available all day. There are 20 generous omelets, from $5 to $7. The sandwiches are complete meals, with potato salad, coleslaw or three-bean salad, reasonably priced at $4-6.50. The zucchini burger is the bargain value — savory squash, almonds, mozzarella, sprouts, tomato, onion, lettuce. Thirteen dinner entrées are served ($5-15).

It's an upfront, amiable stopover, very respectable — and yes, we'll have that extra pickle!

- **Summer Tu-Sun 7—8, Winter 7—7**
- **Beer, wine**
- **Credit cards**
- **Park on street**

Buckhorn Springs

2200 Buckhorn Springs Road
Ashland • **488-2200**

Twenty minutes from Ashland proper, out Highway 66 past Emigrant Lake, you'll see the sign and right-hand turn for Green Springs Power Plant and Buckhorn. The country road winds through thickening forest to the secluded resort. From the parking lot you stroll past the garden, which supplies fresh flowers, herbs, and vegetables for the restaurant (zucchini were threatening to overwhelm the morning we visited). There are rustic cabins nestled under the trees, and Emigrant Creek bubbles nearby.

The kiss of sun for pardon,
The song of the birds for mirth,
One is nearer God's heart in a garden
Than anywhere else on earth.　　　D.F. Gurney

Atop a lush green lawn that seems almost edible rests the main house, originally built in Civil War days, and now listed by the National Registry of Historic Places. Owners Leslie and Bruce Sargent, who have been lovingly restoring the old place, will be pleased to relate its fascinating story.

Inside, the spacious, comfortable entry and dining room are full of light. Reading lamps, easy chairs, and fine antique pieces are set off by the gleaming pine floor. A large fireplace curves along the wall. There's a piano, used by guests now and then.

We'd driven up for Sunday brunch and asked for a seating on the pleasant wood deck which overlooks the garden and creek. Our server obligingly moved our furniture into the shade, where we sat in rare comfort — our benches nicely sun-warmed and a cool breeze on our faces.

 Relaxed ■ country atmosphere!

Brunch ($11) choices that morning included Eggs Benedict, Eggs Arnold (with tofu patty), french toast stuffed with cream cheese and pecans, huevos rancheros, and three omelets — our salmon and herb cheese was particularly tasty. Orders included juice and coffee, as well as banana-nut bread and coffee cake baked fresh by Leslie. The sausages were herby and delicious (especially the tofu version, very light) — a specialty of the chef, Chris Fowler.

In the evenings, Buckhorn offers fixed-price suppers, which vary according to season and Chris's mood. There's always an original vegetarian choice, and either a chicken or fish dish. Meals are served family-style and include appetizer, salad, main course, and vegetables. Reservations are mandatory. Smoking is not permitted inside.

The springs were believed to have magical restorative powers, and the spirit remains. This is a lovely spot for a retreat — your best choice will be Sunday Brunch.

- **Sun brunch April-Dec 10—2**
- **Dinner 6 and 7:30 June 1—Sept 30 (winter at 7 only)**
- **Reservations required**
- **Beer, wine**
- **Credit cards**
- **Park in lot**

C. K. Tiffin's

226 East Main
Medford • **779-0480**

At the tidy entrance to C.K. Tiffin's, the welcome mat is of brightly colored inlaid tile. The spacious, friendly main room is weathered brick and warm golden wood, with pink booths lining the walls and small tables neatly arranged. Overhead, a huge white duct pipe runs along the ceiling next to the circulating fans, looking for all the world like a ghostly, airborne submarine.

Service is cafeteria-style, and the staff bustle cheerfully. At 11:15 one recent morning, attendance was light, but by noon there were few vacant spots. The menu changes weekly, with choices colorfully and artistically displayed; some-one here treats food with loving regard. Sandwiches tower some four or five inches tall, with great slabs of fresh, whole-wheat bread, turkey, onions, tomatoes and sprouts. Salads are exuberant with crisp veggies and fruits. Our soup choice was chicken vegetable, broth thick with onions, pota-toes, peas, carrots, celery and barley, savory with rosemary. To accom-pany it was a dense, dark cornbread (rye flour makes all the difference) which didn't self-destruct on handling. (A delicious meal, under $2!) The condiment tray held yeast, cayenne pepper, liquid aminos, rice vinegar and cilantro sprigs, but we weren't tempted to alter the soup.

The vitality of thought is in adventure...
Alfred North Whitehead

Pastries, homemade that day, included cranberry or cheese scones, poppyseed bran muffins and gorgeous-looking fresh raspberry and strawberry pies, a lemon tart with kiwi, and chocolate vanilla swirl cake. A dollar or two will make you a believer.

Freshness ∎ dedicated service!

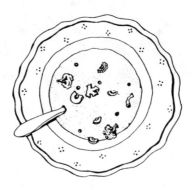

Tiffin's opens at 8 for continental breakfasts. Lunch, the most heavily-attended meal, offers sandwiches, salads and soups, with daily specials such as lemon-tarragon chicken and vegetarian lasagne (about $5). Dinner entrées ($6-9) feature thoughtfully prepared, curried walnut chicken or fettucine with snapper, prawns and scallops. Soup or salad is provided, and freshly steamed vegetables arrive with some dishes.

Retired is being tired twice, I've thought.
First of working, then of not.

Richard Armour

'Tiffin,' we are told, comes from a Hindustani word meaning 'light meal', or the container that carries it. 'C.K.' is Clair Killen, owner (with wife Jenny Windsor) and host. He's an amiable soul with purposeful eyes and a direct, appealing manner. After a career which included work as a machinist, an Esalen therapist and a Silicon Valley salesman, he retired to this area — he tried to — but soon felt stifled. Though he had never worked in the restaurant business, he enjoys risk, and embarked on an ambitious 2-1/2 year program to refurbish the century-old Main Street building. Tiffin's opened in 1991 with a commitment to fresh, natural foods and a determination to treat each visitor as an honored guest. Clair feels that one must have respect for both mind and body — thus the nutritious food and relaxed atmosphere. He pays his staff very well, as he feels they are his most valuable resource. One day, he mused, he'll be completely satisfied with the restaurant, and it will be time for another adventure. When the time comes, he wants to leave the place in confident and caring hands.

- M—F 8-8
- **Beer, wine**
- **Credit cards**
- **Park on street**

Café 24

2510 Highway 66
Ashland • **488-0111**

It's three in the morning and you wake up dreaming of a mound of Belgian waffles. You have a choice: count sheep, raid the kitchen for some stale Oreos — or drive to Café 24. They're Ashland's only 24-hour restaurant, and breakfast is ready around the clock.

The Mother of All Breakfasts is the Lumberjack — a gastronomic sledgehammer at $7. We sat next to a large, wide-eyed woman who said, "I'm a farm gal and I can't begin to eat this." Other selections are more reasonable in both dimension and price. The potatoes are fresh and fried like grandmother still makes them. The biscuits are homemade and the gravy with sausage slices is smooth and not too salty — not an easy trick.

Lunches run $4-7, dinners from $6-11. All are hearty, typical American fare. Avoid the liver and onions, though. It's supposed to be famous but we were unimpressed. On Friday nights, Café 24 features a prime rib special which includes soup or salad, vegetable, potato and rolls for $9, and they're crowded early. Several main selections offer a 'light appetite' option.

He gave her a look you could have poured on a waffle.

Ring Lardner

When we pulled in the other day, we noticed license plates from British Columbia, Minnesota and Nevada — they're just off the freeway, next to the Flagship Inn,

 Round-the-clock meals!

and serve a lot of hungry wanderers. The morning shift — Judy, Betty and Bonnie (manager and baker) — have worked here more than 11 years. Judy's the non-stop talker. She told one fellow behind us to be good or she'd kick him in the seat of his pants — then interrupted herself to yell "Hi ya sweetie" to an incoming regular and slapped down a piece of homemade pie. The jukebox competes with her but doesn't win.

No alcohol is served — this is a family and traveler's place.

Sona si Latine loqueris.

Bumper sticker in lot
(Honk if you speak Latin.)

•24-hours
• No alcohol
• Credit cards
• Park in lot

Campers Cove Restaurant

7900 Hyatt Prairie Road
Hyatt Lake • **482-1201**

Forty minutes from Ashland via Route 66 to Green Springs, take Hyatt Prairie to the left about 4-1/2 miles. Here you'll discover a funny, funky little place called Campers Cove, which hasn't changed all that much since the 1930's. Don't worry about the "**Night Crawlers for Sale**" sign near the picnic tables outside — it doesn't refer to the menu.

Inside, several rooms (one, non-smoking) meander back toward a tiny bar. The sign there says, "Three drink maximum" and it's for real. They do make exceptions for known locals who can make it home on foot.

He is a drunkard who takes more than three glasses, though he be not drunk.　　Epictetus

---

Les McCoy talked to us one morning we'd driven up for breakfast. He and his wife Katie ("the real boss", he says) have run Campers Cove for six years. They are hospitable, humorous, and down-to-earth. Now and then someone suggests they expand the business, add more space, but he and Katie are happy just the way they are, thank you.

There's a full breakfast menu ($2.50-9) heavy on he-man selections but also, we were amused to see, Ultra Slim Fast. Sandwiches and burgers run $3.50-7. Dinner ($7-13) includes liver with onions and an excellent prime rib with horseradish and Yorkshire pudding (Saturday special only).

 **Hearty breakfast ■ excursion!**

Katie joined the conversation as we were paying our bill at the front counter under the watchful eyes of a giant deer head. "Yes," she said, "we make our own pies and rolls. The mashed potatoes are real, none of those flakes. The gravy's real, also. And the biscuits." She began to laugh. "Les is real, too, and so am I."

Eat, drink, and be merry, for tomorrow ye diet.

W. G. Beymer

- **Daily 8—Sundown (Dark-thirty) summer and winter**
- **Full bar**
- **Credit cards**
- **Park in lot**

Chata

1212 South Pacific Highway
Talent • 535-2575

Everytime a friend orders the Mamaliga de Aur (Bread of Gold), which is a staple of Rumanian peasants, her Significant Other worries, "Why don't you get something with meat? The menu says it's just peasant food." But what happy, wonderful, loving food! These fried corncakes are sprinkled with melted cheeses and embraced by a creamy mushroom and wine sauce. Watching her eat this is watching someone in love. (Perhaps her S.O. is jealous.) She can only look at her Mamaliga, lingering over every bite. She doesn't want to share it, and she only wants to dwell on her dreams about it. Or, if she does converse, it's about how fantastic it is. Yes, it must be love.

On the other hand, the roles are reversed when the subject is cabbage rolls, and the S.O. has been known to exhibit all the symptoms of passion. We kept our heads and ordered the obligatory musaka — nothing we can duplicate at home, though we've tried. It's such a clever, complex dish that when it's available we simply pounce. This allowed us time to study the objects of affection. The Limeliters sang a song about Mamaliga, something like, "It will make you dance and sing, it's the very latest thing..." Sounds like giddy infatuation to us! And those cabbage rolls were adorable — ample servings of beef, pork, onions, black olives, white wine with caraway (or you can have the meatless, but why be celibate?), served on rice with red, hearty, sour cream sauce. It makes the lips pucker.

But enough of this silliness. It must be the Limeliter song, which we can't stop humming. Chata used to play this tape in the restaurant, but it's disappeared. A friend has promised to run down a copy for us.

 **Ethnic comfort foods ■ atmosphere!**

Actually, Chata is a serious, sane restaurant. Petite dinners are served for half price plus two dollars. Or you can order appetizers with soup and salad. They make a pickle soup once in awhile that deliciously redefines sweet/sour. The fish soup is authenticated by a friends's recent visit to Russia: "It's just like what was served there."

An idealist is one who, on noticing that a rose smells better than a cabbage, concludes that it will also make better soup.

H. L Mencken

Our sausage appetizer ($4.50) was hot, flavorful, juicy, and served with mouth-watering mustard. The pirozkis, pastries stuffed with cheese topped with sour cream (a dozen for $7), are a little bit of heaven. Entrées include soup or salad, very fresh vegetables, and Chata's own bread. Prices run $8.50 to $15 and there are blackboard specials as well. We wondered about the pizza, which seemed out of place on this menu. Eileen Scowkowski, who runs Chata with husband Josef, explained this pizza version is a Chicago specialty — the Windy City houses the largest Polish population outside of Warsaw.

Desserts are $3.50. The honey custard is proclaimed to be the best, perhaps in the universe, by a local expert who's traveled a lot and should know. The chocolate cake with almonds and potatoes — yes, potatoes! — is rich and hearty and delish.

Reservations are recommended, but if you'll read the discreet sign posted by the door, you'll conclude, as we did, that children are not.

- **Daily 5—9:30**
- **Closed 2 or 3 weeks in January**
- **Reservations recommended**
- **Full bar**
- **Credit cards**
- **Park in lot**

China Station

1950 B Table Rock Road
Medford • **779-2288**

We were over at Mom's, grousing about the truly awful Chinese meal we'd had locally the night before. Bland vegetables, mystery meat that was hard to locate, generic sauce — we went on and on till Mom suggested in her reasonable fashion, "Why don't you go to China Station?"

We couldn't think of a single good reason not to (Mom even offered to sit the baby), so we hurried on over. Somehow this place had slipped our minds since its relocation to Medford four years ago. This restaurant is easy to miss — slow down passing Domino's Pizza (across from where the Big Y used to be), and take a quick right turn by the Coin-Op Laundry. That's it — yellow sign, inscrutable exterior.

Once inside, we're amazed. It's a beautiful little place with rough cedar walls and a deep green carpet. Almost all the work has been hand-done by owners Loren and Juna Brooks. The room is divided between smokers and nons. Honest-to-Buddha Chinese music plays sweetly.

A successful diet begins with chopsticks.

Marion Sasaki

Juna is the chef here. She trained and operated restaurants in Hong Kong, and her dishes reflect the flavors of that colony. As Loren says, "Hong Kong has taken mainland Chinese food and improved upon it."

Ethnic ■ bargain!

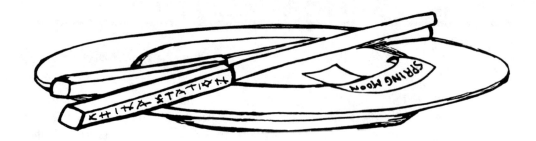

The menu includes regional specialties, Mandarin, Szechuan, Hunan — with several Thai dishes, for good measure. We tried the twice-cooked chicken with cabbage, onions, chili and bean paste ($6), slightly sour and just-right hot. (You can choose your heat level on a scale from 1 to 10 — we chose lucky 7.) Loren recommended the lo mein, thin noodles stir-fried with vegetables ($5.50), and we were glad he did.

On this ordinary, quiet Tuesday in Medford at 7:30, the place was three-quarters full, people were waiting for take-out, and they'd been too busy to erase the lunch specials from the blackboard: pad Thai, moo goo sweet and sour chicken, fried banana with honey. Of the first eight dinner selections, three were already gone. They don't overcook; freshness is a prime concern.

We find the prices here low, portions generous and extremely tasty — this is talented cooking. For dessert, the homemade mango ice cream ($1) provided just the tart-sweet taste we were looking for. China Station is worth rediscovering.

Thanks, Mom!

- Lunch Tu-F 11:30—2:30
- Dinner Tu-Th 5—9, F 5—10, Sat 4—10, Sun 4—9
- Beer, wine, sake
- Credit cards
- Park in lot

Emilia's

Rogue Valley Medical Center
2825 Barnett Road
Medford • **773-6281** (ask for coffee shop)

Are we really recommending hospital food? Well, yes and no. Emilia's is located in the Rogue Valley Medical Center, just off the main entrance, but the food bears no resemblance to the dismal fare normally found in such a setting. Meals are made from scratch, with fresh fruits, vegetables, and nutty whole grains. And check these prices!

Beginning with breakfast, one may savor freshly ground Allann Brothers at 40 cents per cup. Cheese omelets are $4, or add ham and mushrooms for an additional 50 cents. Breakfast plates include hashbrowns and toast — or enjoy the scones and morning-fresh muffins for about a dollar. Fresh fruit and herb teas round out the offerings — and threatened to round us out, too.

Lunch and dinner choices include burgers ($3); fruit, vegetable, or pasta salad ($4); and "Super Sandwiches" ($2-3). The Vegetarian Deli ($3.50) layers cheese, tomatoes, cucumbers, mushrooms, and sour cream dressing on the kind of bread you love. Soups are fresh, hot and hearty. Table flyers alert you to blackboard specials, while the menu lists three dinner entrées: grilled chicken breast, prawns, and beef patty (all $4.50 or under). Save room for the homemade pie — the only thing humble about it is the cost.

The word "bargain" describes Emilia's (seniors receive a 20% discount, too) — also "wholesome", and, need we add, "delicious." Medical staff and visitors keep the place hopping and there's a brisk take-out business. Service can be slow, but it's always friendly and accommodating to special requests. (For example, kids can ask for half sandwiches.) As a long-time employee told us, "We will make things to order." That's a nice touch.

 Bargain ($4.50 or less) ■ informal ■ tasty!

There was indeed an Emilia, one of the founders of the Center's Auxiliary, which operates the restaurant and gift shop. Profits are pooled to offer student scholarships for hospital employees and volunteers, and to defray certain equipment costs — not long ago, a wheelchair van was purchased for the hospital's use.

Eating is not merely a material pleasure.
Eating well gives a spectacular joy to life
and contributes immensely to goodwill
and happy companionship.
It is of great importance to the morale.

Elsa Schiaparelli

When we mentioned listing Emilia's to a friend, she said, "Well, if anything goes wrong, the Emergency Room is just around the corner" — but you can count on things going right. Besides, visiting a hospital when you don't have to is, in this case, an unexpected pleasure.

- **M—F 9-7:30, Weekends 10-5**
- **No alcohol**
- **Credit cards**
- **Park in lot (use main hospital entrance)**

The Good Bean

165 South Oregon Street
Jacksonville • **899-8740**

It may be true that the only permanent thing is change. Wandering Jacksonville one lazy mid-morning last June, we paused before this sign and simply grinned:

"THIS IS USUALLY OUR DAY OFF, BUT SINCE WE HAVE A LITTLE REMODELING TO DO, THE COFFEE IS ON THE HOUSE!"

There were two large rooms with lofty ceilings and comfortable-looking wood and brick accents. The tables had honest-to-goodness reading lamps, the kind with the little pull-chains on them, and magazines were out for browsing. Stacks of lumber, panes of glass, and tools sat about, and extension cords snaked over and through them. A sense of zany optimism and the smell of sawdust prevailed.

The two owners, Mary and Michael Kell, genially pointed out the free coffee and chatted in a somewhat hectic manner about their plans. They'd been doing wholesale coffee business for some time, and the idea was to branch out, serve ten or twelve really special coffees, fine pastries, maybe soups in winter, and — well, they were still organizing. For summer, they were thinking about opening late for the Britt Theater crowd — it would be fun to have live jazz.

We were invited to a grand opening. "It's potluck," Mary explained cheerily, "so bring something vegetarian." "Ummmm," we said. Unfortunately, we missed the party, but we felt sure that a coffee house with free coffee and/or restaurant where you bring your own food probably had a few more surprises up its sleeve.

Do you know on this one block you can buy croissants in five different places? There's one store called 'Bonjour Croissant'. It makes me want to go to Paris and open a store called 'Hello Toast.' Fran Liebowitz

---

 Unique lo-cal dishes ■ original coffees ■ cozy, upbeat ■ bargain

A summer later, we returned. We could smell the rich, heady coffee aroma from across the street. Geraniums cascaded from the front window boxes. Several elf-sized benches had been set up in front with expresso-cup wee tables. Mary greeted us from behind the counter. While she handled a gaggle of tourists, we wandered about. There were an elderly five-foot-tall coffee grinder, a glass-fronted display cabinet with antique books, and dried flowers hanging from the ceiling, all neat and welcoming. The front room was dominated by an immense, unwieldy contraption that Mary enthusiastically identified as their special coffee roaster. It has an after-burner which removes the skin from the bean after roasting, leaving the bean clean and fresh-tasting — thus the "good bean."

On the coffee menu that day were Morning Flight, Ethiopian Mocha Harrar, Guatemalan Antigua, Indian Malabar, Tanzanian Peaberry — the names rolled around in our mouths. Mary has assembled an intriguing assortment of go-withs, which include low-calorie Szechuan curry and low-fat vegetarian quiche, employing skim mozzarella and provolone with no crust, for 120 calories a slice. Their pastry whiz, Diana Lieve, creates sugar-free maple bran and peach bran muffins, chocolate cappucino muffins, and their signature Morning Glories, with carrot, coconut, walnuts, apples, raisins, whole wheat, and non-fat yogurt. These and the heart-shaped English biscuit scones are their best sellers, and can be accompanied in summer by cool soups, cucumber and gazpacho. For sweet sin, there are truffles from McCully House. Prices are low — $1 for soup, muffins for 75 cents.

On the weekends, visiting musicians may play till one in the morning. They're hoping to have poetry readings and Mary mentioned that Bill Cottrell, now 77, who was part of the original Shakespeare company here, may lend his talents. This is a nice and alcohol-free alternative for after theater or after dinner, and the coffee is certainly delicious.

Good communication is as stimulating as black coffee, and just as hard to sleep after. Anne Morrow Lindbergh

---

You'll see the Good Bean name in more and more Valley restaurants, but Mary is cautious about their success and the importance of quality over quantity. "Compared to the coffee whales, we're minnows," she sums it up, "and that's fine with us."

- M-F 7—7, Sat & Sun 7—8
- **open later on weekends with live jazz**
- **No alcohol**
- **No credit cards**
- **Park on street**

Goodtimes

1951 Highway 66
Ashland • **488-1755**

"As you like it" for burger-lovers! Sixteen charbroiled selections in quarter- or half-pound sizes, $2.50-4. True aficionados can customize by adding any of the 22 "extras" from tartar sauce to alfalfa sprouts. The popular Meal Deal (available for lunch or dinner Monday through Friday) features a burger or sandwich with beverage, plus fries or soup or salad, just about $4. Beef boycotters can choose chicken, fish, cheese, BLT, or vegetarian sandwiches.

Goodtimes is now open for breakfast, served 7 to noon, with a full menu including five omelets, homemade biscuits and gravy, and blueberry waffles. Prices are humble.

Jerry Robertson, the second owner of Goodtimes, is justifiably pleased with this homey, friendly, 16-year-old restaurant. The dining room is crowded with booths and some eight tables — but it's bigger than it sounds. An adjoining video game area features two dozen machines. Past this are the five pool tables, with a portrait of W. C. Fields surveying the action.

We lived for days on nothing but food and water.

W. C. Fields

Jerry says their business has always been strong with the locals, and since they've become so family oriented, it's booming. They serve no alcohol and smoking is not permitted. "Family, food, fun," their sign says, and their stated aim is to make "the greatest burgers in the world."

 **Burgers ▪ game rooms ▪ budget!**

47

They're open all year — on holidays, Jerry and his manager run the place by themselves, so his regular staffers can be with their families. He confides that his game rooms often serve as electronic babysitters, but he says it with affection. "If the kids seem too young," he adds, "I just tell the parents."

During long summer evenings, there can be a wait for service. The customers understand because all burgers are made to order and geared to please. Those with a sweet tooth will be happy to find pie and ice cream have recently been added.

As we were leaving, Jerry said, "Oh, almost forgot — we have a jukebox, too — it plays oldies but goodies." We were glad to hear it. Burgers, video games, pool, a jukebox — just like old times — just like Goodtimes.

Jest with life — that's all it's good for.   Voltaire

- **Daily 7-11**
- **No alcohol**
- **Credit cards**
- **Park in lot**

Great American Pizza Company

1606 Ashland Street (Highway 66)
Ashland • 488-7742

The baby was teething and in no mood to be trifled with. Armed with the usual rattles, bottles, diapers, books, change of clothes, juice, and stuffed owl, we took her to the Great American Pizza Company. The front room was compact and tidy, with an immaculate blue carpet. The door at the back was open and beyond it lay paradise. Picnic tables, shade, a redwood tree, and, most stunning of all — a large sandbox filled with pails, shovels, and bright-colored widgets. Aaaah!

Time is a sandpile we run our fingers in. Carl Sandberg

The baby ordered a small plate of shredded tofurella (a mozzarella-type non-dairy cheese) and ate it with a light sprinkle of sand ($free). The weekly special (8-inch, $5; 10-inch, $7; 12-inch, $10) featured asparagus, mushrooms, and shrimp, but after our usual lengthy negotiating session we compromised on a 12-inch split, half vegetarian and half "the works" on sourdough ($11.50). With on-draft Henry's, our happiness was complete. The sausage was spicy, not greasy, the crust was flavorful and bumpy-gold (no styrofoam dough used here), and the veggies were juicy-fresh.

Owners Bud and Maureen Sadler, escapees from Massachusetts, came to Ashland three years ago for its friendliness, country living, and relaxed attitude. They fit right in. Business is good and growing, and they've started home deliveries in Ashland. They make their own sauces (tomato, alfredo, pesto) and crusts (whole wheat and sourdough). You can mix and match 28 toppings from A (almonds, artichokes, anchovies) to Z (zucchini). Calzones, too. If the do-it-yourself process is beyond you, they have combos like the Mediterranean, with

Pizza ■ shade ■ sand!

49

spinach, garlic, artichoke, feta, black olives, and cheese. Medium size is $12. They aim for ingredients low in sodium, fat, and cholesterol, and use no preservatives.

Every hour in the United States, people eat three acres of pizza.

Jane Pauley

The beautiful photos on the walls — mountains, waterfalls, lakes — are from travels the Sadlers have taken over the years. Recently they sent a friend cross-country, loaded up with 35-mm film. We'll be back to see what develops. Oh — and if you're away from town, send the Sadlers a postcard. Next time you're in, it's good for a 10% discount!

- **Sun-Th 11—9, F and Sat 11—10**
- **Beer, wine**
- **Credit cards**
- **Park in lot**

Hamilton House

344 N.E. Terry Lane
Grants Pass • **479-3938**

Just off the freeway, a stone's throw from a major shopping area, you take a short private drive upward to the imposing front of Hamilton House. The flowers sparkle with water and the welcome mat looks brand-new. A comfy padded bench encircles the entryway. A fanciful painting of a large tree begins on the wall and climbs across the ceiling. There's a spotless new player piano tinkling away, and we stare, spellbound.

Doug Hamilton greets us cordially and we're escorted to our table. We pass through a friendly labyrinth of rooms and are seated in an alcove overlooking a tranquil miniature marsh. There is sun-dappled foliage — the pond contains goldfish, we're told, frogs, fish, and turtles — even a few ducks stopped in last year. The ambiance is country American, all pink and green and beautiful bleached wood. There are whimsical murals (our favorite is one of a vigilant sheep in the back room), and the tabletops are strewn with painted flowers. All these are the work of artist Vickie McGallen, who seems like the playful kind of person we'd like to meet.

Glad that I live am I;
That the sky is blue;
Glad for the country lanes,
And the fall of dew.   L. W. Reese

There is patio dining in fine weather, but this evening rain is muttering in the distance. We relax and choose a wine from the quite respectable and

 **Ambiance ■ seafood ■ dinner theater!**

reasonable list ($11-18). For starters, we order the richly layered torta for two, which is delicious and more than ample for three. The fresh oysters, grilled in an extremely light egg batter, are large Puget Sound delicacies, with pure oyster taste and perfect consistency.

He was a bold man who first ate an oyster. Jonathan Swift

The dinner menu is user-friendly. We sample the fine prime rib (sized at $11-15), special each weekend, which is marinated in olive oil, garlic and herbs; and the popular chicken fettucine ($11) with artichoke hearts, vegetables and almonds in a sumptious sauce. Entrées come with soup or salad, fresh vegetable, potatoes, or rice. The specials today are halibut, snapper, salmon, pork Thai noodles, and Cajun seafood stew ($11-13). Desserts are fresh daily and difficult to bypass.

Doug Hamilton sits with us awhile. He grew up in this house, when it was a simple, three-bedroom structure. The family started the restaurant in 1976, when it occupied a much more isolated setting. Through the years the house has quintupled in size, maturing into its present-day stateliness. Doug used to do all the cooking, but success has overcome him, and now he's happy to perform the welcoming duties that are close to his heart.

There are five private rooms upstairs which are used for corporate and civic group meetings. The largest has a banquet capacity of 125 and a stage, and it is here that dinner theater is presented every other month or so. You can enjoy an evening's entertainment and full-course meal (usually salmon or prime rib) for about $20. Watch the local papers for details.

As we are leaving, we notice a small sign near the entrance: "The way to a woman's heart is through the door of a fine restaurant." Well said!

- Daily 5—9
- Reservations recommended
- Full bar
- Credit cards
- Park in lot

Harmony Natural Foods & Café

106 Main Street
Rogue River • 582-3075

A well-loved takeout place of ours (and others as word gets out) is this cheerful, fresh, lilac-accented café. There are three small, flowered tables inside, beside a large Main Street picture window. Outdoor tables are on order.

Proprietor Kathleen Rustrum came to Rogue River from the Central Valley of California, bearing a solid restaurant and management experience. A five-year vegetarian, she was delighted to assume ownership of Harmony and share her natural-foods philosophy with the community. Eventually, she hopes to expand the restaurant space... plans are on simmer.

'Tis not the meat, but 'tis the appetite makes eating a delight. Sir John Suckling

---

The kitchen is open at 11 am but early arrivals are graciously received. The food is so aromatic and interesting that schoolchildren often stop by to stare. Personally, our week-long binges center on sandwiches (about $4) such as the Dilly (Swiss on toasted, sprouted sourdough with tomato, red onion, dill pickles, sprouts and dill) or the Vegetarian Paté (a creamy, peppery paté on toasted, sprouted sourdough with cucumber, tomato, red onion and lettuce). You can also buy the paté for your own late-night snacks. The Creamy Cheeser ($3.50) is layered with cheese, sunflower seeds, cucumber, tomato and sprouts. If you call by 11:00, they can have your takeout ready for lunchtime pickup.

All soups are made daily. Other specials have included cold artichokes with lemon mayonnaise and stuffed, baked potatoes (both under $4), which make

 Vegetarian, natural food ■ takeout violet & green interior!

a light and delicious take-home supper. They're topped with pimento, sautéed mushrooms, green onion and Stripples, a bacon substitute. Many of the new soyproducts, which feature all the taste and texture appeals of meats, without the fat or preservatives, are attractively presented in choices like the grilled tofu steak sandwich with grilled onion — a mouth-watering treat. This is one of the axioms of Harmony: meatless meals can be nutritionally balanced, palate-delighting and completely satisfying.

Kathleen tries to offer a variety of ethnic foods; Mexican, Thai, Middle Eastern, Chinese, which are by nature largely vegetarian and downright delicious. On a recent visit, the Special ($4) was fresh corn-on-the-cob, chilled green bean and tomato salad and fresh-baked bran muffin with currants. There was cheesy zucchini soup, carob truffles and baklava for dessert.

The store is worth a tour. The back room contains a wall of glass jars, full of magic-sounding ingredients: angelica root, black cohosh root, chia seeds, elder flowers, Irish moss, passion flower, butcher's broom, crane's bill root, ground ivy, lemon grass, white willow bark, nettle, blackcurrant leaf, lily of the valley, lovage, and St. John's wort, to name some. There's a tidy library of books for sale that explain all these nutritional mysteries.

The sign outside Harmony says, "**Make every day Earth Day**" and "**Love Mother**". Words to live by.

• M—F 11-6 (café); 9:30 - 6 (store); Sat 10-5:30
• No alcohol
• No credit cards
• Park on street

House of Thai Cuisine

1667 Siskiyou Boulevard
Ashland • 488-2583

When we asked a friend one day what his favorite restaurant was, he named a local trendy eatery specializing in Thai food. Then we mentioned House of Thai and his eyes lit up as he exclaimed, "Ah—now that's authentic Thai food!" House of Thai is sometimes overlooked, but we'd like to share it with you.

It's no flash in the wok — it's a mature, wise place where owner Piengchit Kanjanakaset, known as Jit, "cooks good food that tastes good, so the customer will be happy. I'm really happy when the customer is happy. I do everything for the customer." Her menu, listing 53 food items, including appetizers, soups, salads, pan-fried dishes, meats and vegetables, curries, and house specialties, plus the recently added vegetarian menu, is testament to her desire to accommodate.

For a man seldom thinks with more earnestness of anything than he does of his dinner. Samuel Johnson

---

We find it difficult not to ask for the chicken saté with kicky, creamy peanut sauce or the larb kai: hot and spicy ground chicken, onions, and dried chili. The tohm kha kai is a delicious and very spicy coconut version of Thai chicken soup, guaranteed to cure the common cold or a bored palate. Most dishes are $6 - 10, although you can pay $14 for pla tord rahd prik (whole fish in curry).

One thing we really, really appreciate is that House of Thai delivers. An Ashland friend who was recently housebound with an infant sheds tears of joy when she describes the many evenings House of Thai delivered delicious, hot suppers to

 **Authentic Thai ■ delivery!**

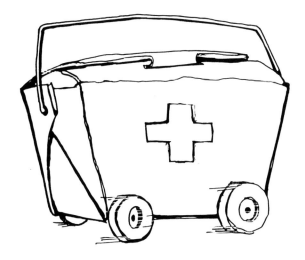

her home — a kind of psychotherapy on wheels. And if you want to get out, it's a lovely place to go. There's a cheerful fountain splashing in a neat garden outside. The interior is colorful and comfortable, and Thai pop music plays jauntily. The staff is friendly and family: Jit's son, daughter, daughter-in-law, and son-in-law. Kids are welcome — get a table near the fish tank and they're mesmerized.

Jit came from Bangkok to America 12 years ago, and spent some time in Hollywood preparing food for the film crowd at the Ruen Pair. These last three years she's been here — we are lucky.

• M-Sat 11-3 and 4:30—10:30, Sun 4:30—9:30
• Beer, wine
• Credit cards
• Park in lot

Hyatt Lake Resort

7979 Hyatt Prairie Road
Hyatt Lake • 482-3331

It was the Fourth of July and a celebration was in order. We took Highway 66 through golden hills to the Hyatt Prairie cutoff (at Greensprings), then 4-1/2 miles to the resort. The restaurant sits atop a modest green rise and commands a stupendous view of the lake.

The town is man's world. But this — country life, is of God.
                                                        Carl Sandberg

A friend thought this was the oldest man-made lake in Oregon, but the Historical Society can't confirm it. They don't even know just who Hyatt was. They do know the lake project was finished in 1922, using horse-drawn scoops called fresnos. When you consider the size of the lake, the fact that construction was completed in a single year seems pretty amazing. We're glad they went to all that trouble. It's a tranquil, beautiful stretch of water with stark grey skeletons of trees left standing to shelter the trout and large-mouth bass.

The restaurant is lined with warm knotty pine. A soft couch and reading chairs flank the old fireplace, where cheerful log fires are laid in winter. This is an intersection for cross-country skiers and other outdoor players. On this 90-degree day, a father was teaching his young son to play checkers. And somebody's grandfather browsed the newspaper while he waited for his to-go order.

Sharon, the local who used to bake the pies, was in for lunch that day and the manager's daughter, who was studying restaurant science, was

 **Lake view!**

doing a summer's homework by serving. (With her smile, she's bound for success.) The special was BBQ pork ribs ($6) so tender they required only a stern look to fall apart. We'll try the roast pork next time — it's slow roasted and environmentally correct, wrapped in lettuce leaves rather than aluminum foil. Two of us had the really fine Hyatt burger ($6). This used to come with onions, but now you must ask. Do so, they're unusually sweet and crisp. (A friend of a friend used to drive from Central Point for these burgers.)

Breakfasts (served till 11) are versatile and inexpensive, with old-fashioned chicken fried steak and eggs plus hashbrowns or pancakes at $7.50. The luncheon favorite is chicken strips with ranch dressing, fries, and garlic bread — under $6. Dinner can be ordered any time after noon, but the baked potatoes won't be ready until 5. There's a nice little entrée list, including halibut with lime ($11). A new menu is being assembled as of this writing, but many of the most popular items will remain.

If they have rhubarb pie and you fail to order it with vanilla ice cream, while eyeing that lovely calm lake, you're going to regret it for the rest of your life. Trust us.

- **M—F 9-8, Sat, Sun 8-8 (Call for winter hours)**
- **No alcohol**
- **Credit cards**
- **Park in lot**

Il Giardino Cucina Italiana

5 Granite Street
Ashland • 488-0816

Una fantasia del cuore — for owners Franco Minitti and Maurizio Contartese, Il Giardino is truly a dream of the heart. Who can say when or where it began? Franco, fluent in Spanish, French, English, and Italian, spent his boyhood on the romantic Riviera. Maurizio, the master chef, comes from Milan, that most energetic of Italian cities — where a standard greeting, "buon lavoro," means "good work." They are a remarkable team.

The two met as fellow employees on a passenger cruise ship — a love boat, as it happened — both married ladies they had met on board. Maurizio settled in LA and Franco in San Francisco, but the friendship endured. There were weekly phone calls and meetings twice a year when they explored the idea of opening a restaurant together. Maurizio had always been fascinated by Oregon, so when Franco planned a visit to his Ashland in-laws, he departed with instructions to look for a place. Veni, vidi, vici! In 1990, the dream became a reality.

We may live without friends; we may live without books; but civilized man cannot live without cooks.

Bulwer-Lytton

Il Giardino means 'the garden' and fresh flowers are only part of the warm welcome here. The double doors under the archway are open, offerings from local artists grace the walls, 'Sixties' Italian music plays softly, and Franco steps forward with a smile. On a shelf above the counter in back, you may admire hefty jars containing Maurizio's latest concoctions — eggplant marinated with Italian peppers, or perhaps goat cheese in olive oil, fragrant with

 **Splendid Italian food ■ atmosphere!**

tarragon and black pepper. Selections vary according to the creative spirit, so if they're not on the menu — just ask.

It's such an at-home place, you might visit the kitchen to see what's simmering, or Franco might join you at your table to make sure all is well. The pasta and dolci are handmade. They keep the ingredients simple and impeccably fresh.

It may be those who do most, dream most. Stephen Leacock

Lunch selections ($4-5) include a primavera (springtime) plate of green and white angelhair pasta with seasonal vegetables in cream sauce. Four pizzas are available, and single slices cost a dollar. At dinner, it's hard to pass up one of the six antipasti, all about $5. Or try the stracciatella (if you smile when you say the word, it's easier to pronounce!). This is a chicken broth with eggs and parmesan — a Roman classic that manages to be both light and rich. It doesn't appear on the menu, but can be whipped up on request. Evening pasta dishes ($7-10) feature the house specialty, black ravioli in a tarragon cream sauce. We're told the pasta's color comes from octopus ink, but don't let that throw you. Dinner plates ($13.50-17.50) of swordfish, veal, king salmon, chicken or steak arrive with salad. And for dessert, if one is able, we'd recommend the tiramisu — a not-too-sweet mixture of chocolate and clouds with a lightning bolt of pure caffeine. Under its influence, some have been known to leap medium-sized buildings.

Buon apetito! Buon lavoro!

- **Lunch M-F 11:30—2**
- **Dinner Daily 5—9 (closed a few weeks in winter)**
- **Reservations suggusted**
- **Beer & wine**
- **Park in lot**

62

Jacksonville Inn Bistro and Bar

175 E. California Street
Jacksonville • **899-1900**

We know that the Jerry Evans' Jacksonville Inn is historic, popular, and wins awards. We know it is elegant, gourmet, and expensive. We know it is in Jacksonville. We also know it has been reviewed so many times, by such prestigious persons and institutions that it has achieved a kind of celestial status. It is not our intention to compete with the experts, but we would like to mention the more modest Bistro located in the back of the Inn, and down the stairs.

The Bistro and Bar have a cave-like feeling, snug and comfortable, cozy with brick and wood. One room holds a table for four and the bar proper with four or five stools. This room opens into another with seven or eight tables — we never really counted. And on weekends we always have to wait, since reservations aren't accepted. In this friendly atmosphere we never mind.

There is nothing which has yet been contrived by man by which so much happiness is produced as by a Tavern.

Samuel Johnson

The paintings on the wall by Applegate resident Leo Meiersdorf invite a smile and a study. (Some of his work is featured at the Bella Union as well — in particular we like the bright paintings of food dishes that are like a child's large cutouts.) These in the Bistro are a jazz theme — his colors are jewel-like. We wonder what he did before he retired.

Over the years we've tried their spanakopita — a spinach-filled pastry with feta cheese, eggs, garlic, and herbs ($7.50). Spinach was never like this when we

Relaxed ■ cozy dining!

were kids. The vegetarian lasagna with fresh vegetables in pesto bechamel sauce (butter, cream, and spices) at $6 makes our mouths water. And their sautéed petrale sole is always ordered by a friend ($9.50). For the carnivorous appetite: sautéed chicken livers ($6), BBQ beef ribs ($8), slow- simmered Italian sausage, beef kabobs, and New York and prime rib sandwiches ($13). There's fettucine with rock shrimp ($9.50) and rich, hot croissants stuffed with salmon, shrimp, and scallops. All dishes are served with fresh vegetables, green salad, and Bistro bread.

We keep comin' back.

• Tu-Sat 2-10, Sun 2-9, M 5-10
• Full bar
• Credit cards
• Park in lot, on street

La Burrita Restaurant & Delicatessen

603 S. Riverside Ave.
Medford • **770-2848**

We usually have enough sense to call and ask about the ceviche when the craving hits — they don't prepare it every day, and when they do it's quickly devoured. But we were having one of those days. The word processor was stuttering, the dog had prickly heat, and everything in the fridge was the same designer color. We found shoes that matched and drove to the air-conditioned oasis of La Burrita. No ceviche.

Pondering this latest setback, we retired to the back room, where a few Negro Modelo beers, chips, and the best salsa in town began to alleviate our distress. The Mexican music was lively, the booths under the hacienda-like roof were cool, and portraits of La Burrita herself smiled slyly down at us. She's a seductive little donkey with a rose between her teeth and a "lighten up, it's only life" expression in her eyes. We lightened.

There was the usual unusual crowd wearing an assortment of shorts, sport jackets, diapers, dresses, jeans, and smiles. On hot afternoons you'll see field workers in the traditional hats of Michoacan.

The special we ordered that night was Camarones Mojo de Ajo (shrimp in double garlic) with hot, moist tortillas, rice, beans, and a tiny cup of special salsa so searing that — well, let's just say that we no longer pluck our eyebrows. All this for $6. The shrimp were perfectly sautéed, spiced, sweet, tender and meaty — the best we've had for months. We split a shredded meat-stuffed tamale for $1.50 — regular menu items top out at $5. For true aficionados, there is menudo.

There's a tienda chiquita in the front room with a variety of cold, imported beer, sweets, salsas, hominy, lard, tortilla presses, cornmeal, soap, and clothing for sale,

 Ceviche ■ prices ■ integrity!

and Mexican videos for rent. Brilliant piñatas flutter overhead. The women who cook and serve have enough English for us gringos. There are other La Burritas in the area, but this one, owned by Octavio and Esther Gitzen since 1985, is first and best.

After all these years, La Burrita still surprises us. Other upscale Mexican places buy ingredients and prepared foods here, and they fold an expensive napkin for you. We like the paper plates and the honest food they hold (and the honest prices we pay).

The louder he talked of his honor, the faster we counted our spoons.

Ralph Waldo Emerson

- M-F 9—9, Weekends 8—9 (Closed only Thanksgiving & Christmas)
- Beer, wine
- No credit cards
- Park in lot

Lithia Park / Winter Café

85 Winburn Way
Ashland • **482-3559**

Just across from the park, there's a two-in-one treat for anyone who hates hovering waiters. From May through Labor Day, this funky little place is called the Lithia Park Café. On the first of October it reopens as the Winter Café, and closes again on April 15, presumably so folks can rest up after tax time. Susan Powell, an upbeat and energetic woman, manages them both, overseeing all recipe preparation and doing most of the cooking herself when autumn rolls around.

The main building used to be a creamery and has hosted many different fast-food places. LPC/WC is now in its third year and we wish them well. There's a cozy little room inside, with a haphazard assortment of tables and booths. Newspapers, magazines, and kids' games are on hand. In summer, this is mercifully air-conditioned. In fine weather the covered outdoor patio is hopping, and take-out for the park is brisk.

This is a great place to bring the kids, and it's a terrific bargain. You have to order at the window and collect your food when called, but when the most expensive menu item is about $5, it's hard to be offended. In summer, the hours are 10-7 every day, and they stay open later for special park events. It's possible to buy a corn dog for your fussy five-year-old, but you'll be pleasantly surprised to encounter delicious cappucino, falafel, an Italian vegetarian sandwich, East Indian crepes, spicy fries (chili powder, cayenne, garlic), and honest, stand-up-and-be-counted salads.

The Winter Café opens at 7 for a dedicated breakfast clientele and closes around 3, except Thursdays, Fridays, and Saturdays, when supper's available till

 **Casual ■ outdoor ■ family ■
■ budget meals with flair!**

10. There's a whole new menu which features comfort foods, such as baked apples, porridge, or potatoes and eggs for breakfast; hearty Susan soups, and curried lentils. On Friday and Saturday nights there's local entertainment indoors, such as folk guitar, and poetry readings one night a week.

And I will fetch a morsel of bread and comfort ye your hearts.

Abraham to angels in Genesis

Whatever the season, whichever café, this food is served with wit and not a little wisdom.

- Seasonal hours (above)
- No alcohol
- Credit cards
- Park in lot or on street

Manna Bakery

358 E. Main
Ashland • 482-5831

Beyond miraculous connotation, manna also means "something of value un-

---

"I was lucky. When God rained manna from heaven, I had a spoon." Peter Drucker

---

expectedly received," like spicy gingersnaps pulled blisteringly fresh from the oven and slapped on top of the display case. Customers scatter momentarily to make room, then lean forward as one to inhale.

So man did eat angel's food. Book of Common Prayer

Manna is a relaxed sunny room with a marbled counter overlooking Main Street. Newspapers and sometimes the New Yorker are scattered about and classical music plays all day. On the walls are soft watercolors, framed newsclips, postcards, and letters from devotees. No smoking, please.

At the heart of Manna has been Hilda Austermuehle, an energetic and beautiful woman whose photos never do her justice. Her first home was above a bakery in Chicago — in spirit she never left that nurturing atmosphere. Gretchen, her daughter, now handles the day-to-day operations, and Hilda stops by once a month or so. The last time we saw her, she was up to her elbows in soapy dishes. We appreciate that. As a friend of ours who owns a market says,. "I always sweep my own floor — if I don't care how the place looks, how can I expect my employees to?"

Atmosphere ■ the New Yorker ■ valley-famous baked goods!

The bakery case is over-full with daily delectables: buttery Scottish shortbread, pioneer muffins, cherry almond or apple struesel tarts. The Narsi David almond cake is named for a famous San Francisco chef, who's traded his recipe for Hilda's. No prices are marked, since changes are made daily and sometimes, it seems, minute-to-minute, but most single-item goodies are $1-1.50. Lunch items include thick, whole wheat or corn crust pizza wedges, or our special love, Greek salad sandwiches ($2). Get there early or they'll be gone. Soups (chilled in summer, including gazpacho) with fresh-baked bread are $2.50. There are warm and cool salads, with ingredients straight from the garden and greenhouse in back.

Man shall not live by bread alone. Matthew 4:4
Bread is the staff of life. Jonathan Swift

Very occasionally, Manna misses the mark and turns out something really strange, like the curry bread we tried once — and we wish the patio area had more usable tables — but our complaints are few and far between.

Just before Christmas, 1990, the lights went out in Ashland and stayed out for a couple of freezing days. Hilda's oven, 1932 vintage, kept on going, and the locals huddled by candlelight in the safe, snug refuge of Manna.

- **Tu—Sat 6-5:30**
- **No alcohol**
- **No credit cards**
- **Park in lot or on street**

Maria's Mexican Kitchen

105 N.E. Mill Street
Grants Pass • **474-2429**

"Cannery Row in Monterey in California is a poem,
a stink, a grating noise, a quality of light, a tone,
a habit, a nostalgia, a dream. Cannery Row is the gathered
and the scattered, tin and iron and rust and splintered wood,
chipped pavement and weedy lots and junk heaps, sardine
canneries of corrugated iron, honky tonks, restaurants..."

Cannery Row, John Steinbeck

Inside, there's a horseshoe-shaped tile counter where everyone congregates, though along the wall are a few mesas chiquitas por dos. On the counter sits a model ship sculpted from Budweiser beer cans. There are curtains with loud flowers, and from the ceiling twinkle little red lights in the shape of chilis. (You may purchase a T-shirt here with these same chilis spelling out "Maria.") A big sign above the cash register says, "Thank you for not smoking, we prefer to die of natural causes," but on the wall just to the left are three velvet pictures of desperados, all with cigarettes clamped in their jaws, smoke billowing. In the kitchen, a cart is stacked perilously with two microwaves and a radio.

We sat and sipped Cokes from glass canning jars, listening to the Beach Boys, eyeing the quirky surroundings and eavesdropping on the other patrons — locals, at that time of day — a frail, elderly couple, a few gals from the office, a father and son. The crowd was homey and gossipy, talking among themselves, to visitors who dropped in, and trading banter with the waitress and Maria, in the kitchen. Her family is from Coahuila, and she has lived in Texas and Santa Barbara before settling here 13 years ago.

 Atmosphere ■ Mexican food ■ bargain!

71

Customers — especially long-distance truckers — may home in on this place from as far away as Canada. They often call ahead with special requests not on the usual menu, or orders for two dozen tamales to go. Local businesses bring their Japanese and Korean visitors, so Maria is building a global fan club.

The battered menu offers a good assortment of tacos, burritos, enchiladas, chimichangas, and quesadillas, as well as menudo and chorizo. We tried the most expensive dish ($6.50), nopalitos — slivered cactus leaves with tender shredded beef and red chili sauce, accompanied by homemade tortillas — delicious. Ask for the hot salsa; their usual variety is tasty but too modest. We dined with Andrew, a special young friend, who worked up a sweat trying to conquer his vegetarian taco salad. Exhausted, he asked to take the rest home.

Next time, we'll come at 6:30. That's when the train goes through, and the whole place rocks and rolls. This restaurant seemed full of good omens for us. As we arrived we found a lucky penny, and as we left, one of our favorite songs was playing: "To every thing, turn, turn, turn, there is a season..." Maria's — great in any season!

- M—Sat 11-8
- Beer, wine
- No credit cards
- Park on street

Markisio's

1764 East McAndrews Road
Medford • **779-8447**

You may have driven by this simple restaurant front in the Crater Corner a hundred times and never noticed anything unusual — an error we're sure you'll want to rectify. Markisio's is a delightful discovery.

The interior is cool-looking and pretty — like a vineyard garden with clusters of grapes and vines hanging through the latticework ceiling. Marie-France Kokkalis, the congenial owner and chef, shared a cup of coffee with us one recent morning and filled us in on a little of the restaurant's backfround. Marie was born in France and married a Greek citizen whose family had been in the restaurant business for generations. She's had experience in Athens and Florida, and moved to this area in 1964, first Ashland, then Medford last year. Markisio is the name of her young, mischievous son, who crept under tables and peek-a-booed around corners while we talked. Daughter Marina also helps out by waitressing.

Marie's dishes reflect the influences of both Southern France and Greece. We started out asking about the Salade Niçoise, expecting a personal note, and got a quick world history lesson. It seems that the Greeks conquered Nice in the fourteen-hundreds, and when they were expelled, the uses of feta cheese, olive oil, squid, anchovies, and spices such as cinnamon and cloves (which the Greeks had by then obtained from India) were left to the fortunate French. Ouzo, the volatile Greek liquor, has the same anise flavor as French pernod, and is used in both countries as an aid in digestion, to counter colds, or for serious celebrations. "The Greeks have a saying that they gave light to the western world," Marie informed us with a shrug and a smile.

We asked about the origins of retsina. "This is maybe a wives' tale," Marie acknowledged. When the Turks occupied Greece in the eighteen-hundreds, the Greeks put their white wine in resin-soaked barrels, figuring the Turks

 Great Greek/French food ■ service!

73

wouldn't care for the taste. Guess again! Somehow this resiny wine goes perfectly with Mediterranean foods.

Fill every glass, for wine inspires us,
And fires us
With courage, love, and joy.   John Gay

At the end of school this June we organized a party to bid farewell to an English exchange teacher, Alison Gilbert, others who were leaving, and to generally welcome the end of the year and beginning of summer. Since no one else seemed focussed enough to choose, we happily made the decision for Markisio's, and on an upbeat evening the fourteen of us assembled — or was it fifteen? — or sixteen? Our reservations weren't quite on the mark, and as unexpected guests appeared, our table was moved, chairs were added, plants and place settings shifted by our gently smiling, impeccably unflappable waiter, Makis. As the orders were given, he patiently answered menu questions, noted special requests, rewrote as we switched orders ("Okay, if you're getting mussaka, I'll change mine to the hot salad. Excuse me, does this mean hot-heat or hot-spicy?"). Only when we reminded him that we'd be needing separate checks did he hesitate — swallow hard — and, smiling still, nod his gracious assent. Any really fine waiter or waitress, it seems to us, must possess tact, athleticism, patience, love of humanity, an excellent memory, stamina, and perhaps above all a sense of humor. Makis definitely has all the above — and is an artist as well.

Look at the copper figure of the fallen Greek soldier on the far wall — and the theater mask, and the helmet — all these are his work.

Many of those present weren't familiar with the dishes on the menu — some had never tried either French or Greek cuisine before, so the arrival of our plates was met with a mixture of curiousity, excitement, and high anxiety. We broke the ice by passing around plates of eggplant dip with pita ($4.50) and kreatopetes ($3), deliciously spiced chopped meat in phyllo. They were demolished in record time, and wide grins greeted the main courses. At our end of the table, flashing forks and cries of "ooh, taste this!" vied with the music and veils of the belly-dancer who gamely dodged our large, chair-shifting presence. The souvlaki (marinated, skewered lamb), moussaka (richly creamed meat and eggplant pie), calamara a la Provencal (squid flamed in cognac, with white wine, tomato, and herbs), and chicken in lemon sauce were pronounced scrumptious and made to quickly disappear. (Entrées are accompanied by pilaf, beautifully seasoned and nutty. They range in price from $7 to $12. Next time we'll try the ratatouille Niçoise casserole with eggplant, bell pepper, tomato, zucchini, and garlic — or the dolmades, stuffed cabbage leaves in lemon-egg sauce — or both!) The retsina was an unexpected favorite and refills were gigglingly requested. It was a wonderful party, full of good spirits, delicious food, adventure, and comradeship — just the kind of thing Marie says is her real reward.

Markisio's serves lunch, too, with all meals under $6, a very nice value. There are beef gyros, vegetarian pita sandwiches, Greek meatballs, chicken pita sandwiches with yogurt-cucumber sauce, as well as scaled-down versions of certain dinner selections such as spanokopeta, or the hot Greek salad with orzo, a rice-shaped pasta, with marinated chicken breast, roasted peppers, and olives.

The belly dancer performs Friday and Saturday nights, but whenever you drop in, the first music you hear may just be the word "yassou" — welcome.

- **M-F 11:30—2, M-Sat 5—8**
- **Limited bar**
- **Credit cards**
- **Park in lot**

Matsukaze Japanese Cuisine

1675 N.E. Seventh Street
Grants Pass • **479-2961**

Entering Matsukaze is like taking a long, deep breath of cool air — then sighing — all at once you're both energized and relaxed. The walls are a soft, calm white, the light fir booths and partitions a muted gold, and the carpet and cushions serene blues. The front windows filter exterior light exactly as a shoji screen would. Lush green plants are scattered throughout. Several tables are shaded by a large white canvas umbrella, with twinkle lights below. Fish nets are draped along walls and ceilings — one holds a long, whimsical, pink paper carp. There are unique Japanese block prints by Walt Padgett and Clifton Karhu. Mellow jazz piano by Phillip Williams plays each Wednesday evening.

Grace Tomashiro, a gently humorous soul, owns Matsukaze along with her sons. By the cash register there's an old black-and-white photo of the boys when they were quite young. The one holding the mop is Jon, who, with brother Anthony, creates the dishes here. They are also responsible for building the beautiful booths and lamps. The family is from Honolulu, where son Peter learned how to cook and inspired the rest of his family. They love Oregon for its spaciousness, wealth of activities, and sense of freedom.

We know a woman who used to work here, and who would generously bring take-out surprises from Matsukaze when she came to call. During this time her popularity was unprecedented, and the invitations flew thick and fast. The menu offers a pleasing assortment of traditional Japanese dishes, but includes a few Korean touches, such as the spicy, marinated short ribs with kim chee (hot pickled cabbage). Grace explained that in Hawaii the cuisine is melting-pot, with Korean, Chinese, and other Asian and South Seas specialties, and the blending of these influences creates an added spark of interest.

One recent dinner began with sushi, prettily presented — cucumber rolls, California rolls with crab and avocado, and plump inari, sweet tofu pockets with

 Cool ambiance ■ warm-hearted Japanese food!

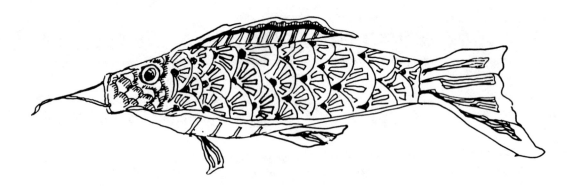

rice and sesame seeds. Selections are $2-3.50. At this point, small plates and bowls began to proliferate. Salad was a crisp selection of greens with a pleasant ginger-garlic dressing. The miso soup seemed impregnable, till the waitress demonstrated how to open the bowl. (Place fingers around the fattest part of the upper bowl, or lid, and squeeze firmly. Lift with care.)

The vegetable tempura ($3.50-6, depending on portion size) was crisply fried in soy oil, and was fresh-tasting and seemingly grease-free. The kalbi ribs and red snapper combination ($11) arrived in a beautiful compartmented wooden box. We'd suggest ordering the fish nitsuke style, simmered in sweet soy. The ribs, very thinly sliced across the bone, were simply fantastic. The Valley had, the day before, earned the dubious honor of being the hottest spot in the country, but by that evening we were enjoying a cool snap of only 90 degrees or so, and in celebration we ordered the beef sukiyaki ($10). This was a delicious, steaming maxi-bowl filled almost to overflowing with seasoned broth, onions, cabbage, broccoli, zucchini, carrots, tiny corn cobs, bamboo shoots, extremely tender meat, tofu, and rice noodles. It was more than our quite willing appetites could conquer. (The sukiyaki also comes in chicken or vegetarian versions.) We finished off nonetheless with green tea ice cream, the perfect closer. It is exactly the same color as the volcanic wasabi (Japanese horseradish) which accompanies the sushi, but is cooled by a cloud of whipped cream.

Also available are chicken deep-fried in a batter of wheat flakes, or simmered in a soy-ginger sauce, teriyaki, grilled mahi-mahi, shrimp, tempura, butterfish, and tonkatsu (pork cutlet). To the left of the front door there's a small raised area where the seating is Japanese-style, and you may grill your own yakiniku, beef with vegetables in sesame-soy, at your table. (This dish is meant for two or more, and costs $15 per person.) We questioned Grace about the authenticity of the seating arrangement, since one need not actually sit with crossed legs flush to the floor — beneath the table is a pit into which legs fit comfortably. We were assured that the Japanese often use this construction because in winter a blanket can be laid across the entire table, brazier included, leaving tea-sippers with toasty warm legs.

To live long
keep a cool head
warm feet.
                                        Japanese proverb

Matsukaze is translated as "breeze through the pines" — a fitting description for this refreshing restaurant.

• M-F 11—2, M-Th 5—9, F, Sat 5—9:30
(in winter, they close a half-hour earlier)
• Beer, wine, sake
• Credit cards
• Park in lot

Mc Cully House Inn

240 California Street
Jacksonville • 899-1942

We were intrigued to learn that owners Patty Groth and Philip Accetta first met as fellow trainees at the CIA. Years went by as the two pursued separate assignments. Phil was headquartered in Washington, D.C., when Patty spied the 1861 McCully mansion a few years ago and realized it would be perfect as a new base of operations. Phil agreed to join forces, and under the unsuspecting noses of Jacksonville, the venture was begun...

Okay, okay — CIA stands for Culinary Institute of America — and the most secret items at McCully are the sauces — we just get carried away now and then!

If anything, the McCully House seems very open and hospitable. Built in the mid-1800's, the mansion has earned its niche on the National Registry of Historic Places, but it's not imposing, just lovingly tended. Somehow the lawn always seems freshly mowed, the furniture just polished, and the flowers arranged moments before you arrive. Service is warm and unhurried, and you'll often find owners and chefs of other local restaurants dining here. In summer, half a dozen tables dot the front lawn. You enter the house from the porch — a gleaming staircase leading to upstairs lodging faces you. The main dining room is to your left, with a fireplace, flowers, a warm, rosy hue. To the right is a smaller room, with antiques and paintings. The waiting area has a cosy couch and fabric wall hangings. The patio area, as of our latest visit, was being glassed in; there will be a full bar here, with a limited number of tables, and a harpist entertaining on Friday evenings. There is no smoking.

Animals feed, man eats; but the man of intellect alone knows how (and where) to eat.   Brillat-Savarin

---

Damned good food ■ ambiance!

Meals are presented with a knowing hand. Lunches feature such salads ($7.50-8) as curried smoked chicken with almonds and fruit, or grilled prawns with spinach. There are sandwiches and specialties like crab and spinach quiche ($8.50). Dinner appetizers ($5-6) might include savory cheesecake with pesto, sundried tomatoes, and garlic; or country paté with blackberry mustard.

At McCully, you can count on the food being inventively prepared, rich and delicious. As one staffer noted, "We're happy to work with people who are watching their diets — no salt, no butter, or whatever — and we always have a vegetarian special. But we're not aiming to be healthy — we're just damned good!" We can certainly vouch for that.

- **Lunch M-Sat 11—2:30, Sun brunch 9:30—2**
- **Dinner daily 5:30—8:30 (call for winter hours)**
- **Reservations suggested**
- **Beer, wine (full bar soon)**
- **Credit cards**
- **Park on street**

Mihama Teriyaki Grill

1253 Siskiyou Boulevard
Ashland • **488-3530**

The Mihama Grill is an unassuming little place that asumes you're in a hurry. We often are, and we jog on in for the surprisingly tasty, reliably prompt, Japanese fare.

Stability is not immobility.   Prince Klemens von Metternich

Just across from Southern Oregon State College, the restaurant draws a sizable student crowd, but on a recent summer afternoon, school was out and the tables were filled with an assortment of busy local folk. You must place your order at the counter, and wait at your table to be served. Take a look around: the decor is eclectic, to say the least. There are some beautiful early Japanese-style pottery pieces in a display case (courtesy of student Wataru Sukiyama), stacks of ancient National Geographics to browse, toy rubber dinosaurs on top of the beer case, Tabasco bottles, and a ten-foot-long koi banner. The room facing the street is a non-smoking area.

There are grilled teriyaki fish entrées each day, such as salmon, snapper, or mahi-mahi ($6-9), served with rice and salad with sesame vinaigrette. Chicken, beef, ginger beef, and tempura vegetable teriyaki plates ($4-4.50) are also available, as well as curry dishes, pork cutlets, fried oysters, and udon (thick noodles in broth) with meat or vegetables ($4). Even burger fans will be content here.

The energetic lady behind the counter is Elizabeth Takeda, who met her husband, Denny, while she was in the Peace Corps on Cook Island. Denny's

 Budget ■ quick, tasty food!

81

family came from a small fishing village near Kugushi on the Sea of Japan, about a hundred miles north of Kyoto — Mihama. The name was first used by his parents, who opened an Asian market and restaurant in Torrance, near the LA airport. Denny's had restaurant experience in Seattle, but this Ashland location is the couple's first joint venture.

After two and a half years, it's earned a solid reputation and a collection of budget-conscious fans — people who value their time, tastebuds, and wallets.

- M-Sat 11—8
- Beer, wine, sake
- No credit cards
- Park in lot

Morrison's Lodge

8500 Galice Road
Merlin • **(800) 826-1963**

Father's Day, the next-to-longest day of the year. An eternity, it seemed, for this was the first true day of summer, when we woke in damp, tangled sheets and struggled through the leaden, 100+ degree hours. By late afternoon, we were repeating ourselves and losing objects still within plain sight — half dead with heat. Our father friend arrived with his pretty young daughter, and we escaped like jailbreakers to the air-conditioned car. Past Rogue River, our spirits lifted, and we took the Merlin exit and swung up the Galice Road, a gradual pine-y climb. As we pulled into the Morrison Resort grounds, we were shocked to find ourselves almost exactly an hour ahead of our reservations. Reluctantly, we disembarked, but ahead were cool, mossy trees and we made our way toward them thankfully.

Anticipation is an aphrodisiac.   Local tavern menu

A path led past a sparkling swimming pool, a storage barn (full of river rafts), and a series of sturdy, Lincoln-log dwellings with Santa-Claus red trim. To our left was a wide, sprinkler-swept green meadow, and we threaded our way down to the banks of the Rogue, sinking into the clover-dotted grass. The first breeze of the day blew back our hair, and brought the unmistakably tantalizing aroma of barbeque. We checked our watches (it had been too hot all day to eat) and inspected the view. There was an Alpine-village feeling about the spot: scarcely-tamed slopes descending rockily to the water, thick stands of pine, the shore grasses dense and brilliantly green. Just before the lodge, the river paused, creating a great serene pond, which wakened into eddies and swift-running little waves a short distance beyond. Fish surfaced lazily for the slow flies and slipped away again. Birds began the evening's conversation. We sprawled and traded stories.

 Excellent food ■ view ■ service ■ value!

Oh, the gallant fisher's life!
It is the best of any;
'Tis full of pleasure, void of strife,
And 'tis beloved by many.

Izzak Walton

At last 7:30 arrived, and we climbed the lodge steps to the deck where we were escorted to our table overlooking the river. (Remember when you come that the best seats are those which allow you to rest your arm and other body parts against a convenient railing.) A waiter hastened, as if some critical element had been left out, to place fresh flowers before us, and large, ice-cold glasses of water appeared. From a nice assortment of wines, we chose the Evesham Wood Chardonnay ($12), which was as expected: spicy, full of pear and apple flavors. Iced tea (expertly made, fresh, crisp, with an undertone of mint) and a peach soda were ordered and appreciatively sipped. Diners (all forms of dress acceptable) settled at tables, and a light clapping of hands drew our attention. The hostess, with the cheery air of a camp counsellor, welcomed us formally, and described the bounty which we were about to receive. Gasps of admiration and/or hunger were heard, and she drew a spontaneous burst of applause.

First, there was the Oriental medley: a light, flaky, oil-free, succulent eggroll, flanked by fresh orange slices, and a single perfect raspberry with a casual toss of sesame seeds on top. We were complimenting the artistry when the Dad in the group leaned over. "Are you going to finish your sesame seeds?" he demanded, licking his fork.

Second, there was salad — crisp lettuces with Mandarin oranges and artichokes.

Third, there were the deservedly famous orange rolls, which were steadily replenished.

Fourth, there were new potatoes.

Fifth, there was zucchini Mexicali, with onion, bell pepper, corn, and cheese.

Sixth, there were The Ribs We'd Been Smelling — thick, saucy pork ribs so tender they leaped from the bone to our waiting forks.

Seventh, there were seconds of everything.

(One of the nicest things about the main courses was that we were handed the platters and bowls and encouraged gracefully to serve one another. We remembered the old Chinese tale: A man asked for a tour of Heaven and Hell. First he was taken into a room with a large banquet table with platters heaped full of food. The diners were seated about 18 inches from the table, and their only implements were very long chopsticks — which could not be maneuvered to feed themselves. The would-be diners were hostile, bickering, and emaciated from lack of food. That was Hell. Next the man was taken into another room. It was exactly the same table, platters brimming with food. Here, however, the diners were plump and happy. The man turned to his guide, puzzling, "What is the difference?" The guide replied, "In Heaven, they serve each other.")

Eighth, there was a chocolate truffle torte with caramel sauce that made us whimper in surrender.

Ninth, there was coffee, and the discreet shedding of shoes and belts.

Tenth, there was the check — $22 apiece for this truly amazing repast. It is only in the last five years that non-lodgers have been able to partake at all. In years past, the Lodge has housed such famous folk as Jimmy Carter and John Wayne, and a host of serious trout fishers. Rafting and hiking are popular pastimes. Nonresidents in parties of eight or more can also visit the Lodge for breakfast (call for details).

Menus change nightly, with a single seating for dinner. Reservations are mandatory. Service is accomplished deftly, with minimum fuss. We kept trying to place that look the waiter had, and driving home, we realized what it was: the face of a friend who waits in pleasant anticipation while you open your birthday present.

• **Dinner daily 7:30 pm**
• **Reservations required**
• **Full bar**
• **Credit cards**
• **Park in lot**

Munchies of Ashland

59 North Main Street
Ashland • **488-2967**

Off Lithia Creek and Guanajuato Way (a few steps from Main Street), take the brick stairs down to this compact, friendly restaurant. In the morning, when baking is underway, you feel as if you've stepped into a sort of heavenly café, dim and rich with the aromas of bread and pies. The pastry case returns you immediately to childhood, since all the offerings seem so outsized — cinnamon rolls seven inches across and four inches high, chocolate cakes nearly a foot tall, and twelve-inch diameter pies with a whimsical dough "M" in the middle of the crust. A friend comes just for the cream pies. As she explains, "With a normal cream pie, you cut it, and the cream just mushes down and vanishes. Here the cream has a life of its own." The other day we bypassed the fresh peach, strawberry, rhubarb, blueberry, and pecan, and took a piece of marionberry home. It was so incredibly dense with fruit that we couldn't resist weighing it: fourteen ounces, ($2.85)!

The best deal of the day is the Eager Beaver Breakfast, served till 11am. For $5, for example, you can feast on eggs with fresh spinach, sausage, onions, and mushrooms, served with homemade cinnamon-raisin-sunflower seed toast, thickly sliced, and what we think are the best breakfast potatoes in town — little red ones, boiled, then seasoned and sautéed with green onion.

He's a great eater, but that's his only skill.   Japanese proverb

---

Full breakfasts at $6-7.50 are served all day. A good idea: you can split an omelet for two with extra spuds and toast for an added $2. A bad idea: charging an additional $1.50 for EggBeaters.

 Baked goods ■ breakfast ■ coziness!

The lunch/dinner menu features 13 Mexican favorites ($5-9), and there are vegetarian renditions at reduced cost. Burgers ($6-7), hot and cold sandwiches ($5-8) and salads ($2-6) are available. Soups are homemade, as are all breads and rolls. There are seasonal specials, such as the summer Indonesian-style pasta salad, or tofu burger Hawaii which we tasted happily.

Munchies is smoke-free. Pleasant, restful watercolors dot the walls. This is a cozy, casual, and comfortable place, well-attended by us locals.

- **Summer: M-Th 9—9, Fri-Sat 8—10, Sun 8—9**
- **Winter: Usually closes at 8**
- **Beer, wine**
- **Credit cards**
- **Park in plaza or city lots**

Nature's Kitchen

412 S. Main Street
Yreka, CA • **(916) 842-1136**

An easy forty-five minutes from Ashland, take the Central Yreka exit on Interstate 5, right to Main, and then left two blocks. You enter Natures's Kitchen through their equal-opportunity health food store where ginger people (male and female) smile from the bakery case. The dining area is another world—absolutely gorgeous. A network of small twinkly lights is interwoven with dozens of hanging plants, forming a lush, green, living ceiling—like a rain forest, as one friend-in-awe described. Weightless white Japanese lanterns float above the tables, and a flute plays hauntingly.

A hungry man is not a free man.   **Adlai Stevenson**

Lunch draws the largest daily crowd, and we know why. On a recent weekday we sampled a sweet and sour vegetable soup (bowl, $2.50), with fresh Jerusalem artichokes, pineapple, carrots, green beans, onion, mushroom, bell pepper, sprouts, brown rice, and tofu in a spicy tomato base. Each spoonful brought a new surprise—like mining for gold. The bread was dense and delicious. (The flour is ground fresh daily from organic Scott Valley wheat, and locally produced honey is used — how sweet this is!) We shared a never-ending magical house salad ($3) which seemed to grow before our very mouths, yielding, from top to bottom, homemade croutons, sunflower seeds, alfalfa sprouts, carrots, tomato, cucumber, garbanzo beans, red-leaf lettuce. (We fully expected clowns to emerge from its depths.) The dressing, sesame garlic, was so extraordinary that we begged for extra rations, twice, and ate the last drops with a spoon. (For the cooking-impaired, they sell this concoction in the store.) The Reuben sandwich (with soup, $4) was made with soy bits—we defy you to tell the difference—and cosmic sauerkraut, along with red potato salad nicely seasoned with dill. We didn't try it this time, but some friends swear they drive here for the coleslaw alone.

 Forest ■ vegetarian ■ philosophy ■ budget!

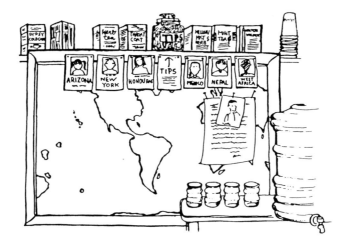

The most expensive tidbit on the menu is less than $5. The star of the breakfast menu, served till 10:30, is a Dutch Baby, a golden, baked popover pancake, served with blueberries and syrup ($3.50). We'll vouch for the lemon bars, too.

This was the first non-smoking restaurant in California. The first owner, Rajiv, had been the soul of the place for fourteen years. He began long before health food was fashionable, against very large odds. In March 1992, travel-lust claimed him and he sold to Jeanne and Gary Brinkman, who were devoted fans.

So many friends had recommended Nature's Kitchen that its joyful aura, delicious food and beauty were almost guaranteed — but there was another surprise in store (literally). This is largely a self-serve enterprise, and tips were never big. The staff decided to pool them, a dime here, a dollar there — and they adopted a child through Save the Children, $20 per month. They posted his photo, word spread, and the tips grew larger. Soon there was another child, then one more — today there are eight, from Nepal to New York.

"Tipping is not a city in China." Flo Harmon, LA waitress
"Tipping is a child in Nepal." Nature's Kitchen

(Such a simple idea, one by one!) Framed by a map of the world, their lovely faces add a special measure of warmth to this remarkable restaurant. Nature's Kitchen is a nice reminder that revolutions start small.

- **M-F 8—4, Sat 9—3**
- **No alcohol**
- **No credit cards**
- **Park on street**

New Sammy's Cowboy Bistro

2210 S. Pacific Highway
Talent • **535-2779**

On first meeting Charlene Rollins, owner/chef, we realized that here was a woman who couldn't say "no" — to a restaurant book. However, we never noticed that she said "yes" either. A recent newspaper review had remarked that Charlene shuns publicity, yet it was clear that she was offended that we didn't know more about her restaurant. While we talked, she punched bread — to punctuate her points of view.

She has a whale of an education in preparing fine foods, and we felt like illiterates being scolded for our lack of experience. After all, we were simply some folks who love eating out and sharing information. Even if several friends hadn't fervently recommended the place, we would have dropped by for the name alone.

It's a naive wine without any breeding, but I think you'll be amused by its presumption.

James Thurber

Yes, there's a Sammy. He's Charlene and Vernon's 6-year-old son and his photos adorn the kitchen. We assume he likes cows since they're all over the walls. As for the 'bistro' part — that's a little trickier. Though they used to run a restaurant in France, and the newspaper dining section chooses to categorize them as French, their menu is written in English, and the dishes, she insists, aren't French. Go figure.

The exterior of Sammy's looks as if a gleeful child had colored it with bright, bold crayons — the flowers alongside the doore even match. Passing through a strange, stark, dim little entranceway, you emerge into the tiny dining room. The

 **Magical food ■ atmosphere!**

91

vivid pastel chairs, dishes, and chubby coffee pots enhance the play-house feeling.

On an evening not long ago, in celebration of a project that was nearing completion, four of us assembled at Sammy's. The feast began with an appetizer of rabbit paté on dense, dark bread triangles, along with prunes steeped in linden tea — an idiosyncratic dish, as most here seem to be — but a very pleasing blend of flavors. Two of us ordered the fixed-price ($25) dinner, which featured tabouleh salad with snap-fresh green beans and slightly spicy grilled prawns, succulent grilled salmon with vegetables in a dill broth, and a mixed fruit shortcake with strawberries, cherries, blueberries, pineapple, and raspberries.

Also served were grilled, marinated rabbit with mushrooms, fava beans, and yellow finn potatoes ($16); and grilled lambchops ($18.50) with sautéed potatoes and greens (mustard or turnip, we believe). The accompanying salad was a crisp, green assortment, and the homemade bread tasted like grandmother's own.

The dining pace was leisurely, with ample time to trade bites, demand further samples from one another, reflect on the ingenuity of the dishes, the spoon-sliceable nature of the meats, the subtlety of the seasonings, and the overall lightness of the meal (by this we mean complete satisfaction, without heaviness). We were stunned, on leaving, to realize that three blissful hours had passed.

Other entrées available that night were chicken breast with spicy couscous and grilled quail with vegetable ragout. The fixed-price menu changes weekly with a la carte choices new each night. Charlene's husband, Vernon, serves and is happy to explain the four-page wine list – he's all in favor of an educated clientele, too. If you leave your wine choice up to him, you'll be perfectly happy. Bottles range from $7-50, with a few available by the glass.

One friend told us that to her, the remarkable thing about Sammy's is the feeling that there's no kitchen in the back — no clatter, no doors opening and shutting, no hustle-bustle. Artistic and delicious meals simply appear as if by magic. But magic, as any mother in an apron can attest, takes a great deal of imagination, forethought, and plain hard work.

We first noticed Sammy's because of a rumor about a two-week wait for dinner reservations in the dead of winter, when so many other Ashland restaurants are whimpering for business. That was a slight exaggeration, but you certainly must plan ahead.

- **W -Sun 5—9**
- **Beer, wine**
- **Reservations required**
- **No credit cards**
- **Park in lot**

North Light Vegetarian Restaurant

130 Main Street
Ashland • 482-9463

North Light is likely to rearrange a few opinions, if you still believe (like a certain Chief Executive we could name) that broccoli is for wimps, that meatless means tasteless, or that tofu is part of some sort of Oriental take-over plot. Guess again.

Tell me what you eat,
and I will tell you what you are.   Brillat-Savin

This authentic vegetarian restaurant has been in Ashland for six years. Gene and Kathryn Casternovia have been serving vegetarian meals since 1970, starting in Washington and Colorado. Though they are the ones who respond when you ask to speak to the owners, this eatery is managed by consensus among the self-employed partners. They guarantee their food 100 percent — meaning that if you don't like the taste, send it back, and they will replace it cheerfully. They want you to be more than happy, to eat well, and to eat vegetarian.

Better is a dinner of herbs where love is,
Than a stalled ox and hatred therewith.   Proverbs 15:17

They offer an "Eat Till You are Content" buffet ($6.50 lunch, $7.50 dinner) that features two soups (one brothy, the other beany), two side dishes, two main dishes, a pasta/potato/green salad and a vegan dish (no dairy). In fact, all

 Vegetarian ■ budget ■ outdoor dining!

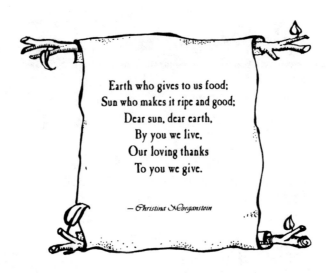

Earth who gives to us food;
Sun who makes it ripe and good;
Dear sun, dear earth,
By you we live,
Our loving thanks
To you we give.

— *Christina Morgenstein*

dishes are vegan unless clearly marked otherwise. Their bottom line is the finest available natural foods prepared with loving care. For example, they use kudzu to thicken their sauces and soup. It's finer and nutritionally superior (and more expensive, about $10 a pound) than cornstarch.

Their menu is a delightful ethnic and budget surprise: whole grain nachos, Greek salad with feta or futa (a feta-style tofu), tortillas, Cajun-style (fiery!) tofu, curry sauté, teriyaki tempeh, tofu fajitas, grain patties, Indian corn pudding, muesli, and soysage (a breakfast soy food), polenta — to name-drop a few. There's a whole section on Mexican specialties plus a kids' menu ($3.50 tops). Entrees are served with soup and salad and average about $7, Mexican specialties average $5. Sandwiches, which include tofu and tempeh burgers, are less than $5. The side-order section is large and varied enough to offer a buffet selection on its own: cheeses, black or pinto beans, rice, guacamole, soba noodles, steamed or grilled vegetables, and more. Breakfast is waffles, pancakes (whole wheat, oats and creamed cashews) served with maple syrup, soy margarine, or butter, grain cereals, and "cruelty-free" eggs (when available) and omelets. Beverages include juices made in Ashland, hot and cold teas, fruit spritzers, and local wines and beers.

Located a half block from the movies and Shakespeare, you can dine al fresco on their patio and watch the Main Street crowds. They don't take reservations, and this is a smoke-free restaurant. If you are talented, audition for their entertainment calendar. They often have local singers and musicians strolling about. The restaurant interior is plant-filled and serene, with aqua and terra-cotta accents, white lace curtains. Plans for the summer of '92 include a late-night Smoothie Bar just off the sidewalk, with light drinks, sandwiches, and pastries for after-theater amblers.

In urging you to try North Light, we'll only warn that it can be habit-forming. Considering alternative addictions you might acquire, not such a bad deal!

- **Daily 8-9 (call for winter hours)**
- **Beer, wine**
- **Credit cards**
- **Park on street or in city lots**

Omar's Restaurant and Bar

1380 Siskiyou Boulevard
Ashland • 482-1281

On Main Street one roasting late summer afternoon, dressed in native garb, we watched an alien (Nebraska license plates) nosedive into a no-parking space in front of us. The passenger, a travel-weary woman of indeterminate age, rolled down the window and beckoned urgently. "We just got in," she said, "and we're hungry. Do you know of a good place to eat?" We took a right-left scan of Main and asked, "What do you want? We've got a little of everything here." She turned to her husband, and they said in union, "Steak." She added quickly, "It doesn't have to be fancy, just good, you understand." Indeed, we did. We whipped out an old envelope and sketched a hasty map. "Look for the camel sign," we advised. With a smile and a wave, they were off to Omar's, the oldest restaurant in town.

We realized the Nebraska lady looked a little like Hazel Hill. We met Hazel, Omar's wife and partner, in 1986, when she was selling real estate. She's a funny, gracious, lovely lady. And she was that and more when she and Omar began to hand-build their restaurant in 1946. They started with a pasture, a bushel of courage, and peck of determination. Over the course of the house-hunting months we spent together, Hazel mused to us about her life: how she and Omar met, worked, and learned the restaurant business from the pro's in Hollywood who catered to the exclusive trade. It never went to their heads.

One of Hazel's remembrances really stands out. Recently she was in the Planning Department on business, waiting her turn, and was approached by Robert Von Der Hellen of Eagle Point. Back in the Fifties, he and his wife, both young folks at the time, would come to the restaurant twice a month for the already famous T-bones. "You probably don't remember me," he began to say — but of course Hazel did. We spoke to him not long ago, and his endorsement was immediate

 **Tradition ■ great food ■ late-night bar!**

97

and heartfelt: "Omar Hill could cook like nobody else before or since in all of Jackson County. Not only was he great at cooking, but also in the selection and aging of that beef. Anybody that ate there would tell you that." To us this is what restaurants are all about — friends, service, good food, and ultimately, memories. Mr. Von Der Hellen's tale was complimentary for them both, because Hazel's memory of her long-ago customers was also vivid.

When we stopped in at Omar's the other day, we weren't surprised to see a prominent Main Sreet restaurateur having lunch. (Certainly he recognizes a class act when he sees one.) He looked right at home, as everyone seems to, at Omars. The room to the right is lined with old-fashioned, cozy wood booths, mirrors, charcoal drawings of tents and camels, windows, and black and white photos from days gone by. Big-band music plays in the background. The larger (smoking permitted) lefthand room is completely surrounded by a deep red comfy bench seat, and the tables at noon always fill up rapidly. This may be the best lunch deal in town, as a friend who spends his work week painting and roofing asserts.

The specials that day included Cajun-style fresh red snapper, seasonal vegetables, and soup or salad; baked lasagne with garlic bread; BBQ turkey with cheddar on a sub roll with soup; and basil fettucini with salad — $5 or less. The soup was cabbage-sausage in a delicious peppery vegetable-based broth. (Before we left we spoke to the chef, who has kids, and gave him a hot tip for toddler dining. In return, we were hoping he'd send us this soup recipe.) The pasta was al dente and beautifully seasoned, and the snapper snapped perfectly. Proportions were just this side of too-much and enticingly arranged — here some cantaloupe wedges, there a drift of zucchini — whoops, a large strawberry.

The dinner steaks ($10-14) are an Ashland tradition, but don't overlook this land-locked location for excellent and fresh seafood. The menu lists calamari piccata ($9) and fresh Pacific oysters ($10-11) and the blackboard specials, New Zealand smoked mussels, butter clams in vermouth and garlic, Chinook salmon with hollandaise, always find a happy audience. The house specialties include chicken livers Madeira and Toad in the Hole, both under $10. Entrees come with whole grain bread, baked potato or rice, and a unique toss-it-yourself salad tray. (We won't even mention the desserts, except to say we succumbed.)

"My people are the people of the dessert," said T.E. Lawrence, picking up his fork. Graffiti on a Pasadena, CA building

---

Omar and Hazel left the business, after nine or ten years, in the capable hands of Al and Betty Jo Brown. In 1974 Rolar Yondorf and Don Mercer took the helm and run it today with Bruce Dwight, who served his apprenticeship in San Francisco and Switzerland. In 46 years, Omar's hasn't lost its focus on quality. Just ask Hazel. As Omar's reigning sweetheart, she celebrated Valentine's Day 1991 there, with a dinner she affirmed was "just as good as the best we ever had" — and that's saying a lot.

There's a nice little bar and lounge (open till 2:30 am every day) in the back room where old and new friends gather. You can have lunch there, and some appetizers and dinner; specials are available too. Relax and enjoy an Omargarita. It's also the only place we know that tracks and posts the local softball and basketball scores.

Omar's always did have heart—it certainly has ours.

- **Lunch M-F 11:30-2**
- **Dinner Sun-Th 5-10 (10:30 on F, Sat)**
- **Full bar**
- **Credit cards**
- **Park in lot**

Pinehurst Inn at Jenny Creek

17250 Highway 66
Ashland • **488-1002**

Lips, however rosy, must be fed. A.B. Cheales

Clouds were massing in the sultry sky as we left for Pinehurst one late afternoon. We were hoping for a good drenching to cool the feverish valley. A half-hour east from Ashland along the pine-enclosed, snaky highway, we rounded a curve and to our right, upslope, a deer calmly watched as we came in sight of Pinehurst. The inn is nestled in a clearing, all tidy in white and green. Originally a waystation for stages on the Applegate Trail, the house was rebuilt in the 1920's. Don and Jean Rowlett purchased it in 1987 and after a year of tender restoration reopened with an outstanding "American fresh" look and taste.

The restaurant is rustic and romantic, with hardwood floors, heavy beams overhead, lace curtains, and table cloths, green and burgundy rugs. The entrance room is filled with high-backed bent-willow chairs. Delia Smith, the Inn's manager, makes dolls and her collection is thoughtfully placed around the room. In the back room there's a massive 1894 wood-burning Home Comfort stove, which provides heat on snowy winter mornings. Tiffany lamps cast a discreet glow, and there are scented, dried flowers on the tables. On the wall is a hazy, soft painting of the surrounding countryside so perfectly captured we took it first to be a window.

The wine book itself is a tactile pleasure: a thick, richly tapestried cover and velvet-lined pages. The dinners are complex in preparation but not fussy — the foods rest in harmony on the plate. Dining is a respectfully prolonged affair, with attentive but leisurely service. Those in a rush will not be happy here.

 Romantic surroundings ■ excursion ■ ■ heart-satisfying cuisine!

Dinner menus change periodically. On Wednesdays and Sundays, pay for one entrée, and the second is free. Dishes are served with soup, salad, and homemade bread, in the $13-26 range. This evening began with mini-loaves of yeasty cornbread, a mildly curried vegetable soup, and a lovely little salad with sorrel and mizuna leaves. We chose the succulent duck with delicate plum sauce and the sautéed salmon in a gorgeous sauce of horseradish and olive oil. For dessert, we shared the lush bread pudding with special peach sauce and fresh berries with cream. A late harvest Riesling dessert wine and bracing coffee completed the feast.

I feel a recipe is only a theme, which an intelligent cook can play each time with a variation.   Madame Benoit

---

We wished at this point only to be adopted, and to live out our years in this blessed environment. That's what is so special about Pinehurst: the dining room may be full but you feel like you are alone and the natural center of attention. Next time we will at least be sensible enough to not wear belts and to book a room. (Pinehurst offers several Bed and Breakfast or Dinner and Bed Specials.) You can fish in this area, hike, horseback ride, or take a jingle-bells sleigh ride in winter — and wait for the Inn's next mealtime.

Pinehurst also serves a country-style, all-you-can-eat breakfast for $8.50 from 8:30-10 Monday through Friday (till 2 on Saturdays). On Sunday there's a varied brunch menu from 8:30 to 2.

- **Daily 5-8:30 (see above for breakfast, brunch hours)**
- **Reservations recommended**
- **Beer, wine**
- **Credit cards**
- **Park in lot**

101

Pongsri's Thai-Chinese Cuisine

1571 N.E. Sixth Street
Grants Pass •479-1345

Tucked into a slightly weird storefront location next door to Mr. X's Swap Shop is the long established, affectionately regarded Pongsri's. Friends of ours, arranging a meeting for lunch or dinner, settle the questions of what day and what time, but "where" is a given — their cars could probably congregate there by themselves!

Pongsri came to the U.S. almost twenty years ago. She and her husband Don von Essen were the pioneers who paved the way for Thai food in the Rogue Valley — may the heavens bless them! Seven years ago the doors opened. The sign said "Thai-Chinese cuisine", so as not to thoroughly dismay the citizenry. Selections today still include such traditional Chinese favorites as chow mein or crab fried rice, but the real nuggets of gold are the dishes from Pongsri's homeland.

Everything is sweetened by risk.   A. Smith

The menu invites a prolonged study. There are 61 entries before the numbering system becomes fitful, starting anew with seafood choices, with combination dinners, and with vegetarian dishes. If you order a Number Eight, it could be fried tofu, tom kah mushroom soup, or shrimp curry, so watch your tongue. Perversely perhaps, we love menus in Thai restaurants. They have another endearing feature we've remarked on over the years — that seldom do we find the names of certain dishes spelled the same from restaurant to restaurant — thus it's masaman (beef curry) in one place, but massamam at Pongsri's. We assume she knows what she's talking about, however the spelling may turn out.

On a recent eventful day, we lunched at Pongsri's and revived over the day's specials: bok choy stir-fried with almonds and water chestnuts ($3); crab rolls

 Thai pioneer ■ bargain!

with shrimp, vegetables and cream cheese, topped with plum sauce; and ho-mok, a spicy concoction of squid, shrimp, fish, cabbage, and coconut milk ($6), served with rice and fresh fruit. We notice that we keep ordering the spicy dishes spicier all the time, but a cardiologist acquaintance assures us it's great for the vascular system. The combination dinners, served with soup or salad, fried rice and wonton, are the most expensive meals at $7, making this restaurant an undisputed bargain. If you fall in love with Pongsri's plum or peanut sauce you can take a jar home. Even with something as hopeless as leftover noodles, the peanut sauce performs last-minute miracles.

We keep meaning to try the mysterious Thai dessert fruits — langan and lamputin, which we were told have a plum/grape taste. The coconut ice cream is homemade and sounds appealing. If just for once we'd order one entrée and then dessert, we'd be glad to report back to you, but don't hold your breath.

The restaurant interior reminds us of photographs we've seen of houseboats along the Thai rivers — tables are sheltered below peaked lattice roofs and enclosed by cosy slatted partitions. Lamps of inverted wicker baskets cast a comforting glow, and tendrils of green leaves twine everywhere. All around are happy voices and the phone is busy with take-out orders.

We once asked Pongsri if her name had a special meaning in the Thai language. We understood it has something to do with flowers, and somethng to do with a bride, or a bridal person — we could picture a bouquet being tossed, but that wasn't quite right, she said. In the end, it seemed untranslatable, but we certainly like the image we arrived at, anyway — something joyful, passed on to another.

- **Tu-Sun 11-9:30 (9 in winter)**
- **Wine, beer**
- **Credit cards**
- **Park in lot**

Primavera Restaurant and Gardens

241-A Hargadine
(below Oregon Cabernet Theater)
Ashland • 488-1994

When Timothy Leary was in Ashland he dined at Primavera and loved it. Were the mushrooms magic that night? We don't doubt it. He especially admired the portrait of Einstein, a fellow eccentric/genius, which used to lean casually against the vivid walls of the gallery front room of Primavera. Art exhibits come and go, but are always worth the view. The ambiance of the restaurant is New York chic, with black tablecloths, white napery, gold columns. A full bar extends along the right side. Symphony music plays gracefully. The back room is larger, elegant, rich and earthy, lined with Charlene Hall murals, inspired by the movement and costumes from Ballets Russes posters. Before the first course, your senses are awake and intrigued.

The setting sun, and music at the close,
as the last taste of sweets, is sweetest last,
writ in remembrance, more than things long last.

Shakespeare

Owner/chef Tracy Darling chose her life's passion early — by the time she was nine, she donned the family apron and would regularly fall asleep with not a teddy bear, but a cookbook clutched in her arms. She's devised an eclectic continental menu of uncommon freshness and variety. The Dijon mustard, she concedes, does come from France, but almost everything else is created in-house: pasta, bread, condiments, ice cream, mascarpone — and they smoke their own salmon and meats.

 Scrumptious food ■ garden dining ■ art-full interior!

104

The menus change weekly. Bistro selections are available beginning at 4 pm, and may include such delectables as rock shrimp in filo with smoked salmon, chives, and creme fraiche; or pasta salad with smoked chicken, each $7; or baked ricotta with olives, $5. The full menu is served starting at 5 pm. A recent evening's starters offered a crostini sampler with three toppings (olive, tuna peppercorn mousse, and goat cheese with rosemary and lemon), Caesar salad, and parsley pesto mushrooms with broth and croutons, all about $6. Entrees with salad and bread ($14.50-19) included grilled beef filet with mustard rosemary sauce and buttermilk, onion, and garlic mashed potatoes; whitefish and clams in tomato herb broth; and bollito misto, a smoky garlic-fragrant broth of chicken, duck, pork, and vegetables. Usually available on weekends is a four-course, fixed-price dinner, at $23. This is extremely sophisticated cuisine — prices are fair.

Reservations are a must. There is a gem-like little garden to the rear with a few tables, where you feel embraced by flowers and trees. Expect to spend an hour to an hour and a half for this extraordinary visual and culinary experience.

- **Daily 4—10 (closed January)**
- **Reservations required**
- **Full bar**
- **Credit cards**
- **Park on street or city lot**

R-Haus Restaurant

2140 Rogue River Highway
Grants Pass • **474-3335**

By the side of the road in front of the restaurant, there's a tiny lighted building with a picture window which houses a miniature antique dining area, complete with tiny stove, gilded butterflies on the wall, two places set at the table, with pink linen and crystal. At Christmas, appropriately dressed mannikins occupy the chairs. This is your introduction to R-Haus, a shaded lodge set well back from the highway, across the clipped green lawn, under the cool, overarching trees.

Visiting this restaurant is always a little like going to see our somewhat eccentric, well-off old auntie. Once inside, it takes a moment for your eyes to adjust to the dimness, but when they do, the visual feast begins. In the entry room, there's a stiff-necked sofa, a three-foot-high radio, a Fullotone record-player, and a full-throated grandfather clock. Everywhere are dark, worn wood, richly patterned red carpets, flowery wallpaper, and antique treasures: gleaming cabinets, a fat-legged piano, elderly Singer sewing machines. Upstairs (the smoking area) there's a friendly, horseshoe-shaped bar, and, among other pieces, an S-shaped double chair. The idea seems to be that a couple could occupy basically the same space, but face opposite directions, so that only their forearms are in danger of touching. (There must be a special name for this piece of furniture, but we haven't discovered it yet.) Nearby is a stout metal washing machine that looks like it weighs a ton — it has a wringer, which we learned early to respect at Grandma's house. There's a slot machine, circa 1948, a dressmaker's form with a Sunday-best frock displayed, Tiffany lamps — and more. Beyond the bar area and large windows is a second-story deck, overlooking the back lawn which slopes down to the river — just the kind of hill we used to love to roll down. There's a wonderful white gazebo, red roses, and a weeping willow. It all seems sort of Alice-Through-the-Looking-Glass.

… Soon her eye fell on a little glass box that was lying under the table: she opened it, and found in it a very small cake, on which the words "**EAT ME**" were beautifully marked in currants.

Lewis Carroll

 Antique-buff's paradise ■ excellent food ■ ■ river view!

106

Larry and Jan Hillis own R-Haus and are responsible for the impressive antique collection, as well as the extensive menu of very tasty fare. Lunch offers several sandwiches, salads, and pasta dishes ($5-7). Each day there's a new deep-dish quiche with a Dijon-mustard-blessed crust, served with salad or soup for $5, or moist frittatas of spinach and mushrooms or seafood. Entrées are varied and moderate in price.

Dinner selections include a lighter-fare group, including many with low salt, fat, and cholesterol, such as the fresh poached Oregon cod in a basil-tomato sauce ($8). Portions are smaller than those on the regular menu. Fresh seafood and pasta dishes highlight the main course list. The star of the show is bouillabaisse, that traditional vessel of buried treasure: fresh clams, mussels, prawns, crab legs, scallops, and lobster in a heady saffron broth. We recently sampled the scallops ($13) with champagne, garlic, and shallots in a buter cream sauce. This sounded almost too rich, but was surprisingly light, with scallops perfectly cooked, tender, and flavorful, presented with the deservedly renowned vegetable-rich pecan rice and a sprightly salad with honey-mustard dressing. Pasta selections wed fettucine, linguini, and angel-hair with prawns, crab, steak, mixed seafood and, improbably, chicken in bourbon (we have yet to try this). These entrées are $12.50-17.50. Traditionalists will be pleased with the prime rib, pork or lamb chops, and chicken cordon bleu.

Wines are plentiful, with certain selections available each month at bargain prices. Service is prompt and good-natured. When we asked to take home the day's excellent potato soup for a friend, we were warned that R-Haus really didn't have the correct containers. When we insisted, the accommodating server presented us with a heavily taped container which read in large letters, "This side up! Hot soup! Careful!" We had to promise to put it on the floor of the car or in the trunk before he anxiously let us go. The soup made it home just fine and was delicious, but we had a little trouble breaking in to it!

R-Haus may look like our relative's ancient home, but (sorry, Auntie Edith!) the cuisine here is first class.

- Sun-Fri 11—2, Daily 5—10
- Reservations suggested
- Full bar
- Credit cards
- Park in lot

Renate's Alpine Restaurant & Bar

1011 Spring Street
Medford • 772-2481

When we look back on our footloose days, we notice we had a few stumbles along the way, so it's always particularly sweet when we remember being at the right place at the right time. It was a plain and simple fluke we happened to be in Munich when Octoberfest began one year. Overnight, a vast new city full of hangar-sized beer tents arose on a field just outside town. ("Munchen" the natives called it — our kind of name!) It seemed half the world came to the party. The weissbeer foamed, the bands oompah-pahed, the crowd sang along in several languages, and rosy-cheeked waitresses dispensed sausages, overflowing mugs, and the largest radishes we've ever seen. They still had their little pink tails on, and a carving contest giddily ensued. In no time the table was overrun with little red radish rats. Ahh — those were the days...

Now we console ourselves at the Alpine. We first met Renate Koehler five or six years ago when we lived in Medford and awoke each morning with a recurring dream of her Kaiser rolls. We'd load up the car with the homework we hadn't quite finished, and arrive at the Alpine when the doors swung open. Breakfast was Renate's lively face, her good, strong coffee, eggs over easy, homemade sausage, chunky herbed potatoes, and **those** Kaiser rolls. And if we got up too late for breakfast, our dreams were satisfied with Renate's lunch burger served on her Kaiser rolls and fries ($4). After all these years we're still fans, and we're not alone.

Vintage 1991 gave a Best International nod to Renate's potato pancakes, sausage, red cabbage, and of course the famous Kaisers. We give the ambiance of Alpine a high rating too; it's spacious, welcoming, and full of good cheer. There are coats of arms, beer steins, cuckoo clocks, tapestries, and — see if you can spot the Indian elephant. There's also entertainment on Fridays and Saturdays with some wicked gypsy tunes, and lately Renate's been organizing some European nights. Call to ask about them — they've been great fun.

 Kaiser rolls ■ sausages ■ Renate!

Or go anytime for the down-to-earth, hearty continental fare. Weekend reservations are a good idea. The Speisekarte (dinner menu) offers schnitzel a la Vienna, sauerbraten, Hungarian goulash, peppersteak, weisswurst, and spicy Hunter's sausage. Entrées ($6-12) are served with combinations of spaetzle, red cabbage, potato, dumplings, German pancakes, or fresh vegetables. There's a joyous assortment of European and Pacific Northwest beers, several on tap, and desserts are fresh nightly.

But most of all there's Renate, a Renaissance woman if we've ever met one — impeccably dressed, whatever the time or circumstances — baker, sausage maker, hostess, tapestry-weaver, antique collector, waitress, chef extraordinaire, entrepreneur, always with a smile. You must see to believe. We believe.

If you get a good woman, you get the finest thing on earth.   E.F. Burton

---

- M 11-2:30, Tu-Th 11-2:30, 4:30-9, F-Sat 9-2:30, 5:30-9, Sun 9-2:30
- Reservations suggested on weekends
- Full bar
- Credit cards
- Park in lot

Rogue Brewery & Public House

31-B Water Street
Ashland • 488-5061

We were tired, hungry and indecisive —shall we try this place? Do they serve food? Will it be any good? Then we overheard a couple on the deck as they settled down at one of the umbrella-ed picnic tables with their backgammon board.

"Goody," he said happily, "we got the same table as last year." With that inadvertent recommendation, we chose our table and went down the Tom Sawyeresque ramp to place our order —it's strictly self-serve. We ate wonderful bangers ($5) with their special beer-mustard, kraut and ale-bread, as we sipped our Rogue Goldens.

"I'd rather have a bottle in front of me, than a frontal lobotomy." Grafitti

---

From the deck we admired three young fellows shooting hoops just below, in the shade. There wasn't a lot of netting left, but they weren't hitting it anyway. The basketball is courtesy of the brewery, and they replace the netting when it's invisible. Inside, other games are available. There's no smoking allowed. Kids are welcome for meals before 9 pm.

Rogue Golden, Ashland Amber and Rogue Shakespeare Stout head the brew list. There's wine, too, sarsparilla, cream soda and juices. The menu offers a few sandwiches (under $6). Pizza by the pie starts at $9 with 10 possible toppings or by the slice at $2 each. There are smaller snacks, too. On summer weekends there's usually BBQ —smoked sausages, meats and tofu burgers from Soy Works.

 Local brew ■ snacks ■ late night hours ■ ■ great restroom!

Manager Patrick Couchman tells us that tours of the brewery can be conducted when there's a lull, and reminded us about the restroom. Go in, turn off the light, and the night sky will glow at you from walls and ceiling. It's the most popular seat in the house!

There's entertainment Friday and Saturday, beginning around 7:30 (8:30 in winter) 'til midnight, from string quartets to folk to jazz. Stop by. You'll find the chaps as friendly as any in a Goode Olde English Pub.

- **Daily 12-12, call for winter hours**
- **Beer & wine**
- **Credit cards**
- **Park in back or public lot**

Samovar Family Restaurant & Bakery

101 E. Main Street
Medford • **779-4967**

Thank heavens we didn't hit anyone! There we were, on a tear down Main Street, intent on our errand list, when the cry went up — "Samovar! A new restaurant!" Heedless of traffic, we made a suicidal right turn onto Front, killed the engine, and hopped out. The door was locked, but we beat on the glass and made beseeching faces till we were admitted. What a lovely restaurant — it has the feel of a European sidewalk café moved indoors — there are old-fashioned street lights, a long planter box of greenery, and pastel ice-cream parlor tables and chairs. There is a weathered brick wall, apricot hues, tall windows, an immaculate air. The staff assured us they would open the next day, and we left in a state of thrilled anticipation.

The discovery of a new dish does more for human happiness than the discovery of a new star. Brillat-Savarin

We arrived promptly at 12:45, to a nearly full house. The place had only been open for two weeks, but a dedicated throng munched happily. Two couples at a nearby table spoke intimately in English and Russian, laughing and gesturing humorously as we tried to listen in and concentrate on the alluring menu selections. A table of five was sharing a bit of this, a taste of that — all mmmmmm-ing with pleasure. The waiter passed through with a dessert tray and for a moment, a hush fell about us. The party he offered his treasure to consisted of three women, and there were four impossible-to-choose-between pastries. Cries of anguish ensued.

We had our difficulties, too, with selections — everything looked wonderful, but our questions confounded the anxious-to-please but English-hesitant waiter. He summoned the owner for relief and translation. Jenna (Yevgeniya Tenyashvili) is

 Teriffic Russian & Middle Eastern ■ bargain!

a lovely, dark-haired lady with a generous smile and uncanny green eyes. She came and went, working at a just-under-breakneck pace, while graciously trying to resolve our inquiries. Her family is from Baku, in the Azerbaijan province which used to belong to the Soviet Union. Her brother, a graphic artist, first settled in New York City, then moved to the Rogue Valley twelve years ago, in search of a clean, small, family-oriented community. Jenna, a physician in her homeland, along with her husband Gogi (engineer and baker), set up residence here two years ago. They spent six months restoring the restaurant interior, and by now have two dozen relatives living and working in the area. Jenna also used to be a nutritionist in Baku. We noted, "And now you still use food to heal people?" She laughed and said, "Yes."

We chose for our first adventure the pelmeni ($4.50), described as a frozen, poached pastry with meat. "Frozen?" we inquired. Jenna shrugged, "Siberian," she answered. What arrived were small, hexagonal ravioli look-alikes, with a scrumptious ground turkey, cilantro and parsley filling — like dumplings, but springy and weightless. For dipping, there was sour cream and tomato relish.

The plate was beautifully assembled with fresh fruit wedges, broccoli and bell pepper. We kept making the *mmmm* noise. We also sampled the borscht ($2), which is served hot here, laced with potato, onion, tomato, cilantro, cabbage and beets, and crowned with a little floating cloud of sour cream. With this comes Gogi's own fragrant, dense rye bread. We were overcome.

Still to try are the Green Mountain salad with yogurt dressing ($2), piroshki (65 cents), meat- or cheese-filled flaky pies, kebabs of beef, chicken or lamb ($4.50 -6.50), various pilaf dishes, stuffed cabbage, Russian blintzes ($3) with meat, cheese or potatoes—and the pastries! Among the offerings that day were bulka (75 cents), Russian sweet rolls, puffy and aromatic. Some (for the children, Jenna explained) were in playful animal shapes. Lunch has been an instant winner and Jenna may open in the future for breakfast coffee and pastries, and (we hope) for dinner as well.

'Out of sight, out of mind' when translated into Russian by computer, then back into English, became 'invisible maniac'.... Arthur Calder-Marshall

---

There's a huge, gleaming samovar in the front window. Webster defines this as "a metal urn with a spigot, used to boil water for tea." Jenna is more precise, in her impressive English. "It's a symbol, hospitality. Big pot, hot, hot tea. You must wait to boil, wait to drink. Everyone together, talking, around samovar. Relaxing. Friendship."

We couldn't have said it better.

•M-F 11-3 (No dinners, yet)
• No alcohol, yet
• No credit cards, yet
• Park on street

Sengthong's

434 Main Street
Etna, CA • (916) 467-5668

"My van's out of the shop and running great," a special friend reported jubilantly. "How about treating me to dinner and I'll drive." It was an offer we couldn't refuse. We made a hasty phone call and soon we were crossing the border into California. The sun beamed, the engine purred, and at Yreka we left the freeway and headed west on Highway 3. Thirty miles of gentle farmland later, we pulled into Etna. It was a little early for dinner, so we strolled here and there, enjoying the peaceful old homes, watching kids on bikes, dogs napping in the shade.

Etna, population 350 or so, was named for the Aetna Flour Mills, and during gold rush days became known as Rough and Ready. When the town reverted to its original name, the "A" was discarded, and eventually the mill left town, too. A tiny Main Street lives on, with several of the original buildings still standing. We passed a quilt shop, a paperback bookrack on the sidewalk (25 cents each, or free after 5 pm), a women's economic opportunity center, and posters on the windows announcing an upcoming cowboy poetry contest. In the middle of the block was Sengthong's.

We'd been hearing tantalizing rumors about this place, but nothing prepared us for the reality. The rooms are cozy, softly lighted, and snug. There are photographs from a century long past, and unusual ceramic pieces created by owner Don Phelps and local artist friends. Sengthong (pronounced Sang-tong), Don's wife, is a Vietnamese chef whose family developed their extraordinary culinary skills in Thailand. Her menu includes Thai, Laotian, and Vietnamese specialties, with prices (including salad and bread) from $8 to $25.

We ordered the Etna Pale Ale on tap. This is from California's northernmost brewery. It can be toured while you're in the area (call 916-467-5277. The dinner

 Sensational ethnic food ■ excursion!

salad was quickly demolished. It was accompanied by Sengthong's own dressing, so delicious it's bottled and sells out in Ashland stores (you might try the Farmers Market in Phoenix).

None of the fish dishes was available that evening, as Sengthong is fanatical about freshness, and that day's supply had been judged inadequate. Don advises calling if you're really set on seafood — it's a good idea to have reservations, anyway. By the time our dinners arrived, the tables were nearly full. We ordered the hot Thai beef with mint, carrots, red onion, cabbage, and peanuts, served with sticky rice and a wicked red sauce ($12). The traditional way to eat this is to line your fingers with rice and use the resulting rice magnet to snare the other ingredients. (For those whose mothers told them never to play with their food, this style of eating is a revengeful delight!)

---

*They say fingers were made before forks,
and hands before knives.* J. Swift

The Vietnamese spring rolls ($11) are another hands-on treat. The crispy rice-paper rolls are stuffed with shrimp, chicken and sprouts, and deep-fried in a magic potion that leaves no trace of oil. The proper way to consume these delicasies is to lay them in a lettuce leaf, add green onions, basil, mint, noodles, cucumber, parsley, cilantro, and the tangy peanut-carrot sauce, roll into a sort of tamale, and plunge.

We were not at all hungry when we arrived, but the only things we didn't eat that night were our napkins. Sengthong took a few minutes from the bustling kitchen to accept our raves. She's a graceful, composed, and beautiful woman, who seems utterly at home in her incongruous surroundings, and very modest about her remarkable restaurant.

Appetite comes with eating. Rabelais

Our only regret was that we'd postponed this excursion too long. We hope you'll learn from our mistake!

• W, Th, Sun 5—8:30, F, Sat 5—9
• Reservations suggested
• Beer, wine
• No credit cards
• Park on street

Serge's

4617 Stewart Springs Road
Weed, CA • (916) 938-1251, (800) 322-9223

One day in the country is worth a month in town. C. Rossetti

About a year ago we were talking to the then-owner of Nature's Kitchen in Yreka, gentle Rajiv, and he was raving about a brand-new restaurant he'd discovered out in the middle of nowhere — Serge's. "Who knows how long he'll last out there," mused Rajiv, "but the man is a genius and that's where I go to eat."

We recently made our long-overdue pilgrimage across the border. Just before Weed (about an hour and twenty minutes from Ashland), we left Interstate 5 at the Stewart Springs Road exit and followed the winding country lane uphill. The road dead-ends at a massive wooden gate, which gave us the impression that a medieval city might lie just beyond. Instead, there was a modest brown lodge with a mossy, shingled roof. The interior has a pretty room with a large, cosy fireplace and ten tables. It was slightly chilly, but we couldn't turn down a place on the deck. Pines and cedars soared beside us, and just below there was a small covered bridge, where an all-male party was evidently bonding at a long table. Park's Creek splashed over the boulders beneath.

There's music in the sighing of a reed;
There's music in the gushing of a rill;
There's music in all things, if men had ears:
Their earth is but an echo of the spheres.

Lord Byron

 Restful, invigorating atmosphere ■
■ gourmet French cuisine!

Henry Stewart founded Stewart Mineral Springs in 1875 after a healing experience he enjoyed here, crediting the miracle to the pure water and serene surroundings. Today, the extensive grounds house facilities for workshops and seminars. Serge Margot first provided chef services for private retreats, and last year opened the restaurant for a grateful public. He brings 17 years of French cooking experience to the task.

The dinners are complex and ours were sinfully rich. This is no place for a dieter of unsteady resolve. We began with appetizers ($4.50) of Caesar salad (the genuine article!) and an airy scallop mousse. The banana squash soup deserved a careful savoring. It arrived with small, dense, delicious rolls that reminded us of palm-sized, smooth river stones. Entrées included soup or salad and vegetables (crisp zucchini and scalloped potatoes to cherish, that night), and were modestly priced at $9-15. Flavors are not submerged here. The trout was tart with lemon, and the flaky, moist salmon was sassy with dill. The chicken breast teased the palate with hints of apple and smoky brandy, and the steak with pepper cream sauce made us gasp with pleasure. (This was ordered medium rare, and arrived exquisitely tender and perfectly cooked — they must employ someone full-time with a stopwatch.) From the dessert tray we selected the raspberry-chocolate cake, and carried it away for a midnight feast.

The restaurant is also open for Sunday brunch ($4.50-7), with such wakeners as smoked salmon eggs Benedict, shrimp, and garden omelets.

Serge's makes a delightful excursion to celebrate a special occasion or simply the company of friends.

- **Spring, Fall: Th-Sat 5—10, Sun brunch 10—2**
- **Reservations recommended**
- **Wine, beer**
- **Credit cards**
- **Park in lot**

Sunshine Natural Foods Café

128 Southwest H Street
Grants Pass • **474-5044**

This sweet, peppy little neighborhood café is humming with life on a mid-week lunch hour not long ago. Inside, every table seems to contain groups of friends, chatting away, or sprawled comfortably sipping coffee after their meals. There are pleasant booths, ice-cream-parlor tables and chairs, a high white ceiling, and a health-food store in back.

A sort of happy Seventies air prevails — behind the counter, the Birkenstocks dance back and forth, a few customers sport abundant ponytails and luxuriant beards, and Joni Mitchell lilts in the background. Our friendly waitress has the most marvelous electric hair we've ever seen — red curls spiralling and sproinging joyfully.

A good life is sunshine in the house.   William Thackery

The soup today is corn chowder ($2.50), thick with fresh-off-the-cob kernels and other perfectly simmered fresh vegetables. We share a Vegecstasy sandwich, gorgeously sloppy with avocado, carrots, sprouts, artichoke hearts, red onion, tomato, soy cheese, and olives, and a tempeh burger with all the goodies, each about $5. If you're by yourself or have kids, the half-sandwich alternatives may be a good bet; there are 19 to choose from. The day's specials include tempeh enchiladas, soup, salad, bread, and tea or coffee for $5, or a well-seasoned half-bean/half-rice dish for $3. Vegetarian Mexican dishes are $3-5, and feature tacos, burritos, and quesadillas. Breakfast is offered from 10, with a limited menu of bagels, pastries, juice, and hot drinks.

**Casual vegetarian fare ■
■ out-of-this-world cheesecake!**

Nancy Norman is the determined owner of Sunshine. She's been open for business in Grants Pass for about two and a half years; the store is a more recent addition.

Do not, repeat, do not bypass the cheesecake! It may be the best we've ever had the privilege to encounter. Instead of the weary, Oreo-like exterior we're used to, which turns into glue on the roof of the mouth, this creation has a crisp, hearty crust of oats, nuts, sunflower seeds, and secrets we can't identify. It makes a perfect counterpoint to the thick, creamy, honeyed filling — heaven on earth!

- M-F 10—7, Sat 10—5 (call for winter hours)
- Wine, beer
- No credit cards
- Park on street

INDEX

AL FRESCO

Alex's
Applegate River Ranch House
Arbor House
Bel Di's
Britt Landing
Buckhorn
Hamilton House
Il Giardino
McCully
Morrison's
North Light
Primavera
R-Haus
Rogue Brewery
Serge's

AMBIENCE

Alex's
Applegate River Ranch House
Arbor House
Bel Di's
Britt Landing
Buckhorn
Chata
Hamilton House
Il Giardino
Jacksonville Inn Bistro
Markisio's
Matsukaze
Mc Cully House
Morrison's
New Sammy's
Pinehurst
Primavera
Renate's Alpine
R-Haus
Sengthong's
Serge's

BARGAINS (top dollar noted)

Ashland Soy Works	$5
Bagel Man	$4
Beasy's (openers/closers)	$8
Breadboard	$6
C.K. Tiffin's	$9
China Station	$8
Emilia's	$4.50
Good Bean	$3
Goodtimes	$5
Harmony	$5
La Burrita	$6
Lithia Park/Winter Café	$5
Mihama	$9
Munchies	$9
North Light	$8
Nature's Kitchen	$4.50
Pongsri's	$10
Rogue Brewery	$9
Samovar	$6.50
Sunshine Café	$5

BREAKFAST

Beckie's
Breadboard
Brothers'
Campers Cove
Café 24
Emilia's
Goodtimes
Hyatt Lake Resort
Lithia Park/Winter Café
Munchies
Nature's Kitchen
North Light
Pinehurst
Renate's Alpine

BRUNCH, SUNDAY

Britt Landing
Buckhorn
Mc Cully
Pinehurst
Renate's Alpine
Serge's

COFFEE AND PASTRY

Bagel Man
Beckie's
Bloomsbury
Brothers'
C.K. Tiffin's
Café 24
Emilia's
Good Bean
Hyatt Lake Resort
Lithia Park/Winter Café
Manna
Munchies
Nature's Kitchen
North Light
Samovar
Sunshine

ETHNIC

Arbor House - International
Bagel Man - English, New York
Brothers' - Varied
Chata - Mid-European
China Station - Chinese and Thai
House of Thai - Thai
Il Giardino - Italian
La Burrita - Mexican

ETHNIC, CONTINUED

Markisio's - French/Greek
Maria's - Mexican
Matsukaze - Japnese/Korean
Mihama's - Japanese/Far Eastern
North Light - Varied
Renate's Alpine - German
Samovar - Russian/Middle Eastern
Sengthong's - Vietnamese,
                          Laotian, Thai
Serge's - French

EXCURSIONS

Applegate River Ranch House
Beckie's
Bel Di's
Buckhorn
Campers Cove
Hyatt Lake Resort
Morrison's
Nature's Kitchen
Pinehurst
Sengthong's
Serge's

FAMILY

(comfortable with kids)
Applegate River Ranch House
Arbor House
Ashland Soy Works
Bagel Man
Beasy's
Beckie's
Breadboard
Britt Landing

FAMILY, CONTINUED
(comfortable with kids)
Brothers'
Buckhorn
C.K. Tiffin's
Café 24
Campers Cove
China Station
Emilia's
Goodtimes
Great American Pizza
Hamilton House
Harmony
House of Thai
Hyatt Lake Resort
La Burrita
Lithia Park/Winter Café
Mihama
Morrison's
Munchies
Nature's Kitchen
North Light
Pongsri's
Renate's Alpine
Sunshine Café

FINE DINING
Applegate River Ranch House
Arbor House
Bel Di's
Il Giardino
Markisio's
Mc Cully House
Morrison's
New Sammy's
Pinehurst Inn

FINE DINING, CONTINUED
Primavera
Serge's

LATE HOURS
Alex's
Bloomsbury
Café 24
Good Bean
North Light
Omar's
Rogue Brewery

LOCATION
City, state, near Shakespeare (N.S.)
Crater Lake, Ashland Lakes

ASHLAND:
Alex's - **N.S.**
Ashland Soy Works
Bagel Man
Beasy's - **N.S.**
Bloomsbury - **N.S.**
Breadboard
Brother's - **N.S.**
Buckhorn
Café 24
Goodtimes
Great American Pizza
House of Thai
Il Giardino - **N.S.**
Lithia Park/Winter Café
Mihama
Munchies - **N.S.**
North Light - **N.S.**
Omar's
Primavera - **N.S.**
Rogue Brewery - **N.S.**

LOCATION, CONTINUED

APPLEGATE
Applegate River Ranch House

GRANTS PASS
Hamilton House
Maria's
Matsukaze
Morrison's (Merlin)
Pongsri's
R-Haus
Sunshine

JACKSONVILLE
Britt Landing
Good Bean
Jacksonville Inn Bistro
Mc Cully House

LAKE REGION EAST OF ASHLAND
Campers Cove
Hyatt Lake
Pinehurst Inn

MEDFORD
C.K. Tiffin's
China Station
Emilia's
La Burrita
Markisio's
Renate's Alpine
Samovar

LOCATION, CONTINUED

NORTHERN CALIFORNIA, Just off I-5
Nature's Kitchen - Yreka
Sengthong's - Etna
Serge's - Weed

ROGUE RIVER, The City
Harmony

SHADY COVE (Crater Lake Route)
Bel Di's

TALENT
Arbor House
Chata
New Sammy's

UNION CREEK (Crater Lake Route)
Beckie's Café

NO ALCOHOL
Ashland Soy Works
Bagel Man
Bloomsbury
Breadboard
Café 24
Emilia's
Good Bean
Goodtimes
Harmony
Lithia Park/Winter Café
Manna
Nature's Kitchen
Samovar

VEGETARIAN

**(At least one vegetarian
plate offered)**

Alex's
Applegate River Ranch House
Arbor House
Ashland Soy Works (vegetarian only)
Bagel Man
Beckie's Café
Bel Di's
Bloomsbury
Britt Landing
Brother's
Buckhorn
C.K. Tiffin's
Campers Cove
Chata
China Station
Emilia's
Good Bean
Goodtimes
Great Amerian Pizza
Hamilton House
Harmony (vegetarian only)
House of Thai
Hyatt Lake
Il Giardino
La Burrita
Maria's
Markisio's

VEGETARIAN, CONTINUED

Matsukaze
Munchies
Nature's Kitchen (vegetarian only)
North Light (vegetarian only)
Pinehurst (call ahead)
Pongsri's
Primavera
Samovar
Sengthong's
Sunshine Café (mostly vegetarian)

VIEW

Alex's
Applegate River Ranch House
Bel Di's
Britt Landing
Buckhorn
Hyatt Lake
Morrison's
R-Haus
Serge's

READER/DINER RESPONSE FORM:

Please give us your opinions on the restaurants you visit that are special to you, what you like about their food, their prices, service, decor, location, atmosphere, etc., or comments about this book.

Name of Restaurant: _____

City, State:_____

Comments: _____

_____

_____

_____

_____

_____

_____

_____

Your name: _____
        (Anonymous is okay, but we've put **ourselves** on the line)

Phone or address: _____

Mail to: Alexandra Productions, P.O. Box 861, Gold Hill, OR 97525

ON THE EATIN' PATH

A very biased guide dining guide
to the Rogue Valley and beyond.

52 weeks • 52 adventures
Amaya • Grillo • Schneider

Number of copies requested: _____

To be sent to:

Name: _____

Address: _____

City, State, Zip: _____

Enclose $12 per copy. Checks only. Postage & handling
is included. Allow ten days.

Mail to: Alexandra Productions
   P.O. Box 861
   Gold Hill, OR 97525